LITERALLY PHOTOS OF COFFEE FOR
YOUR COFFEE TABLE.

PHOTOS BY EMMA RODRIGUEZ

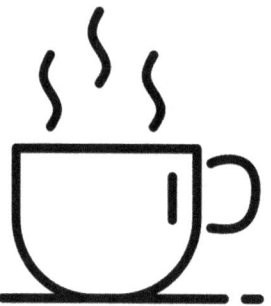

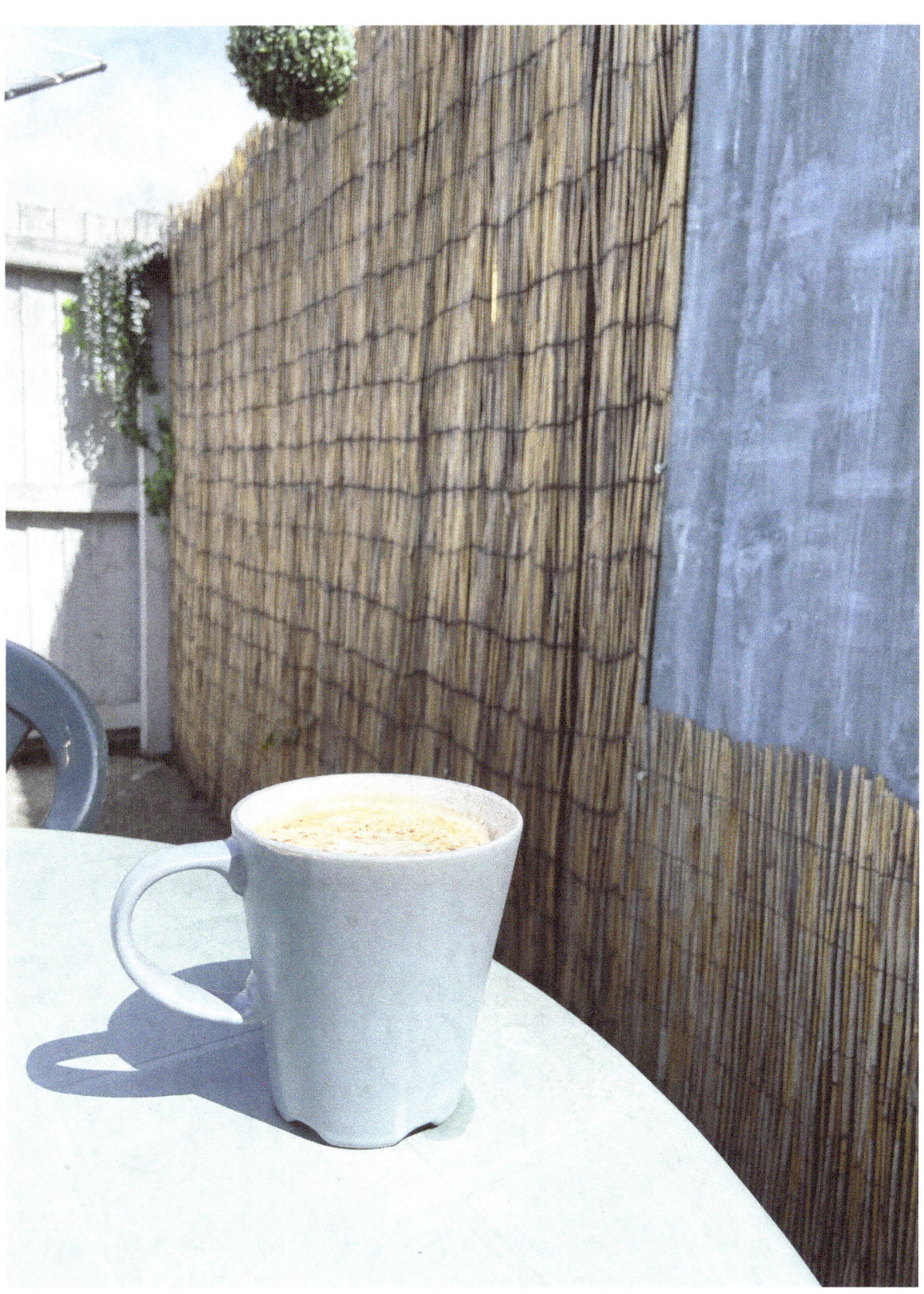

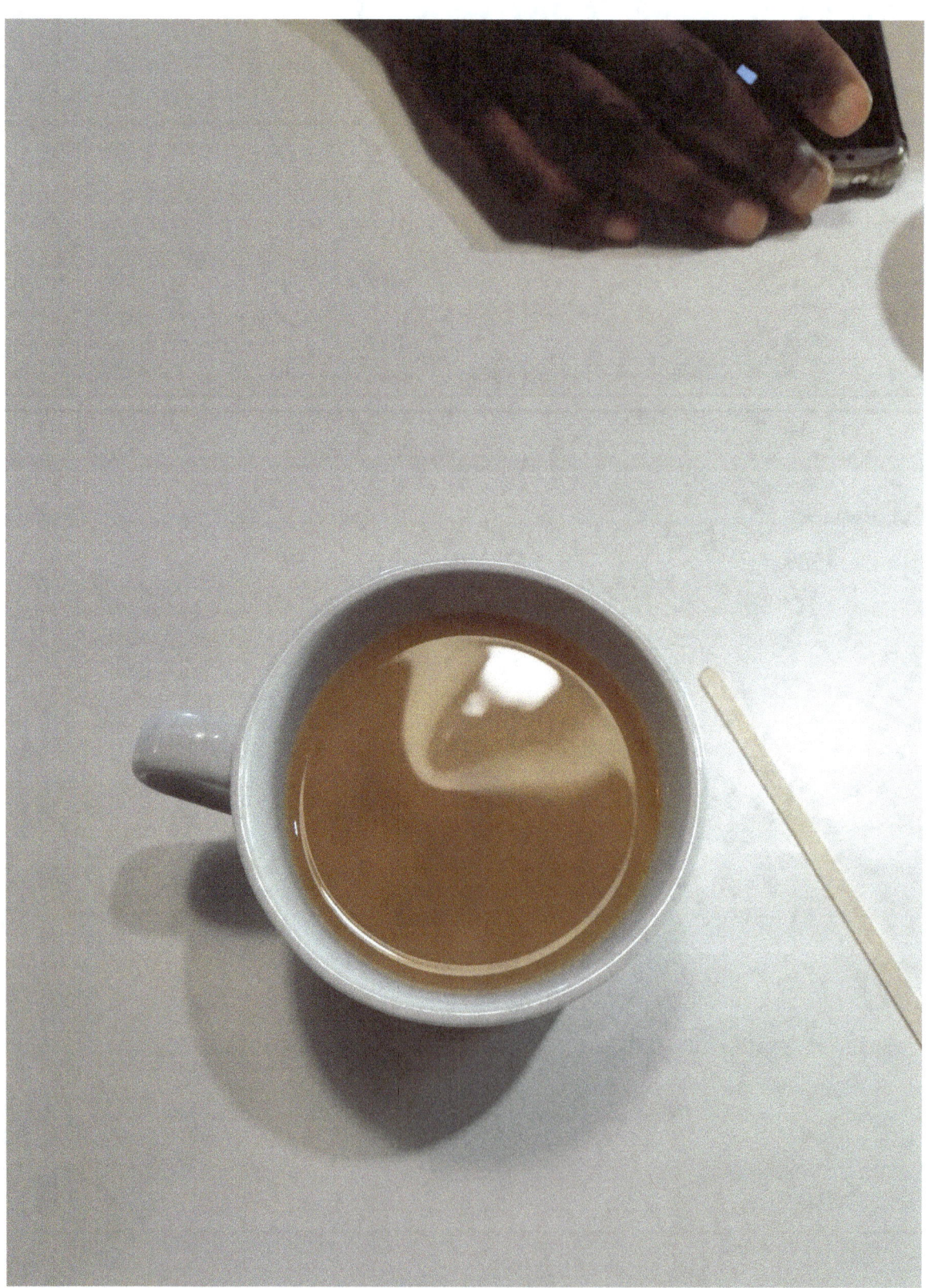

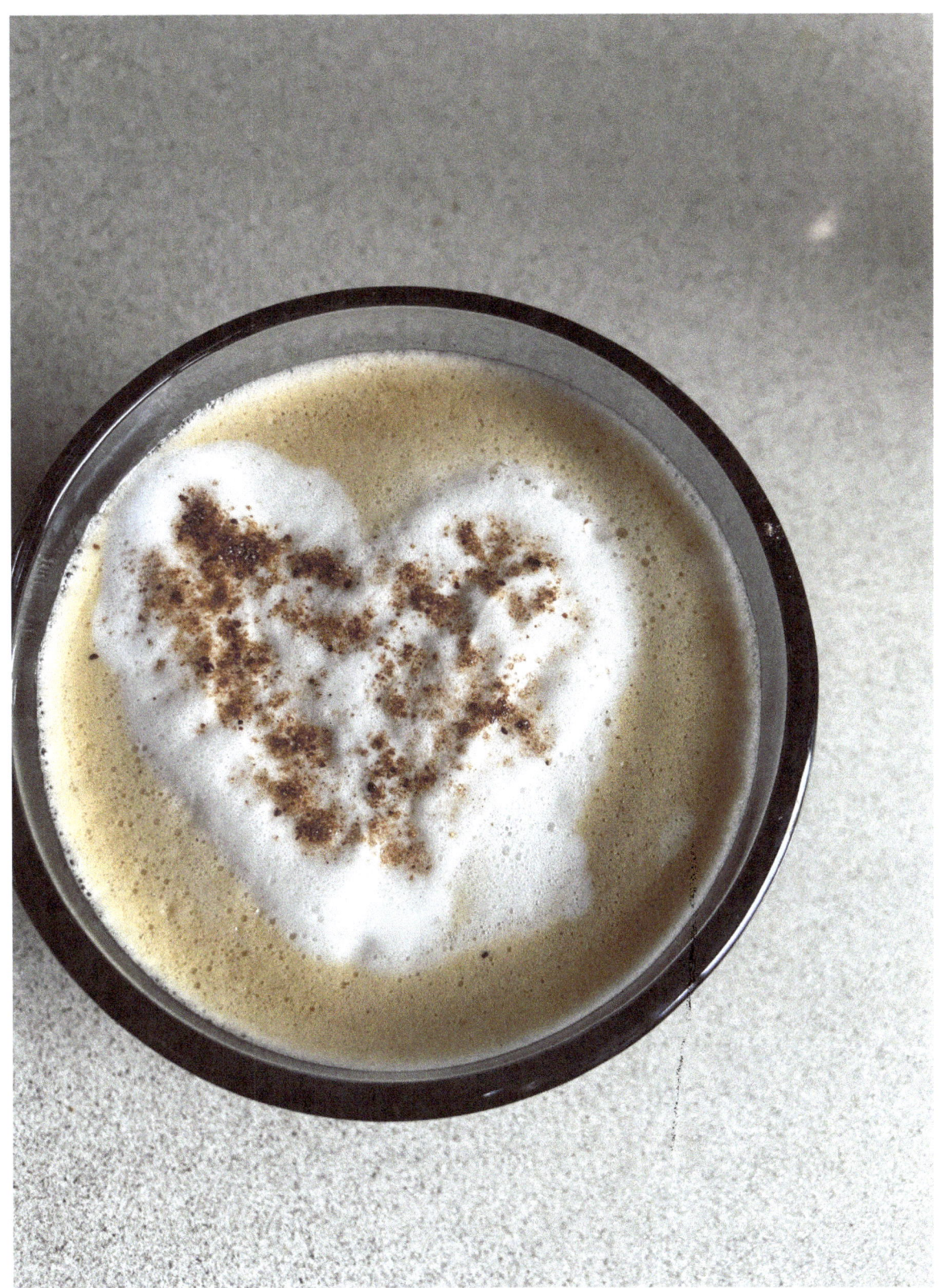

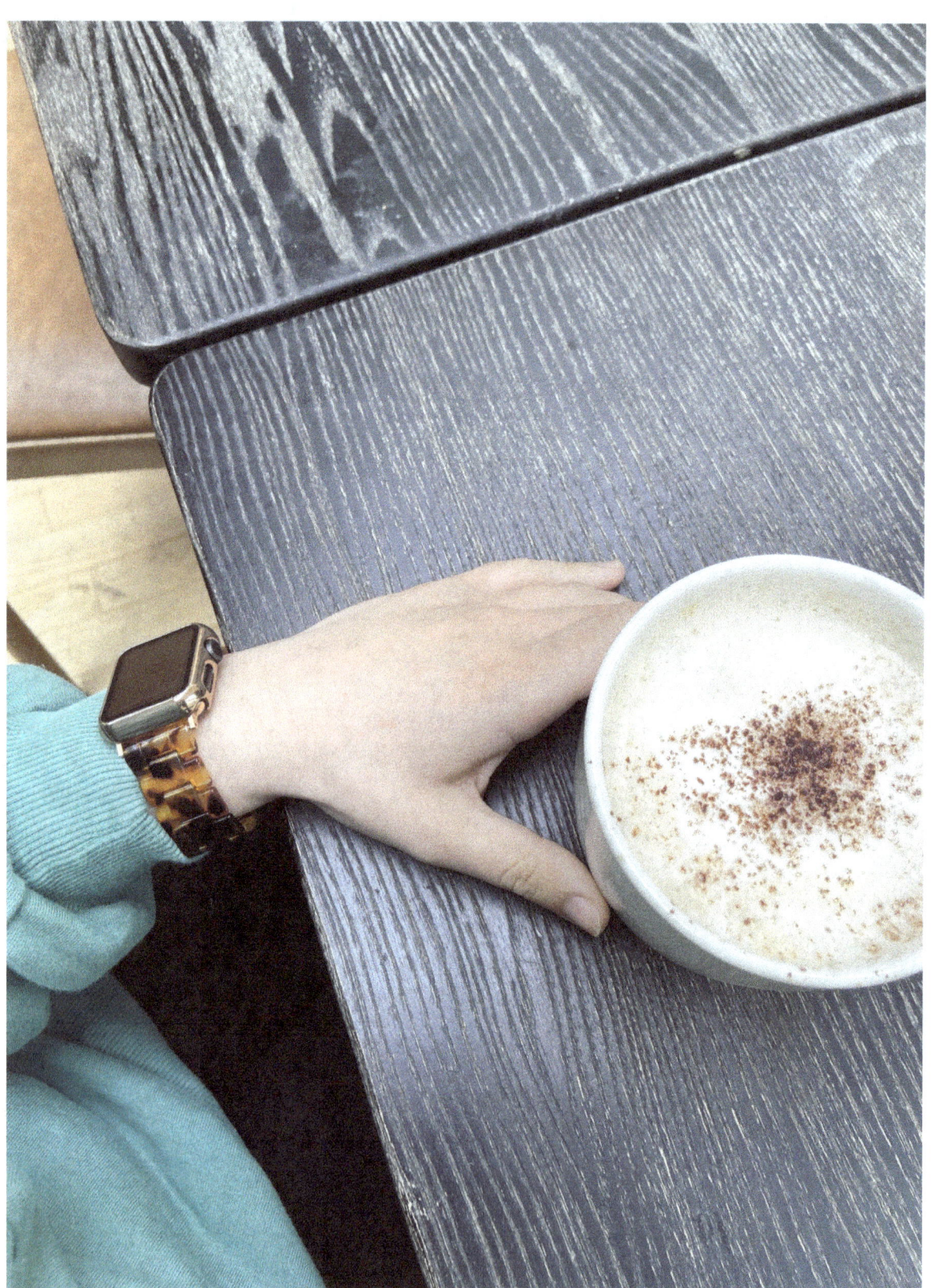

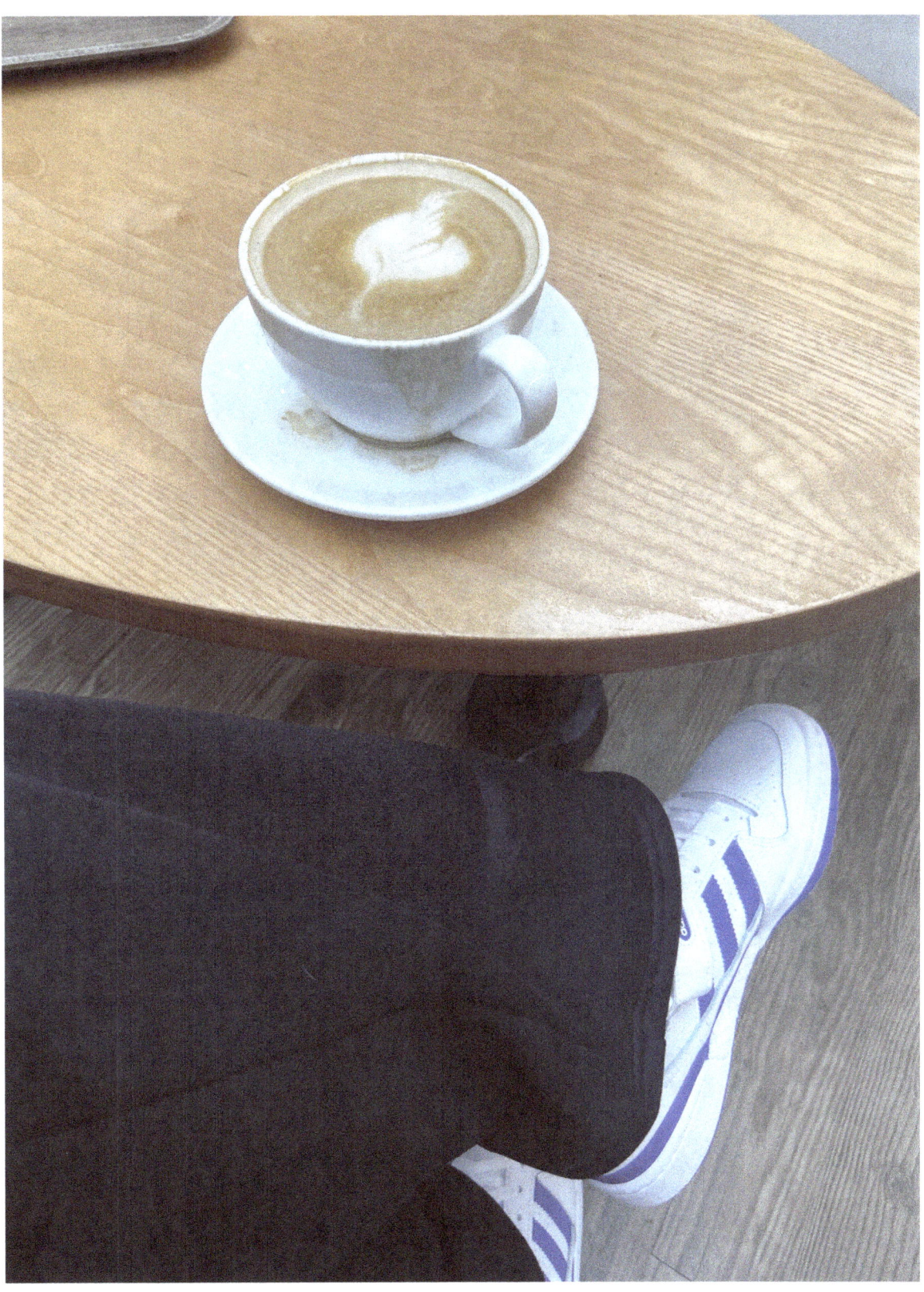

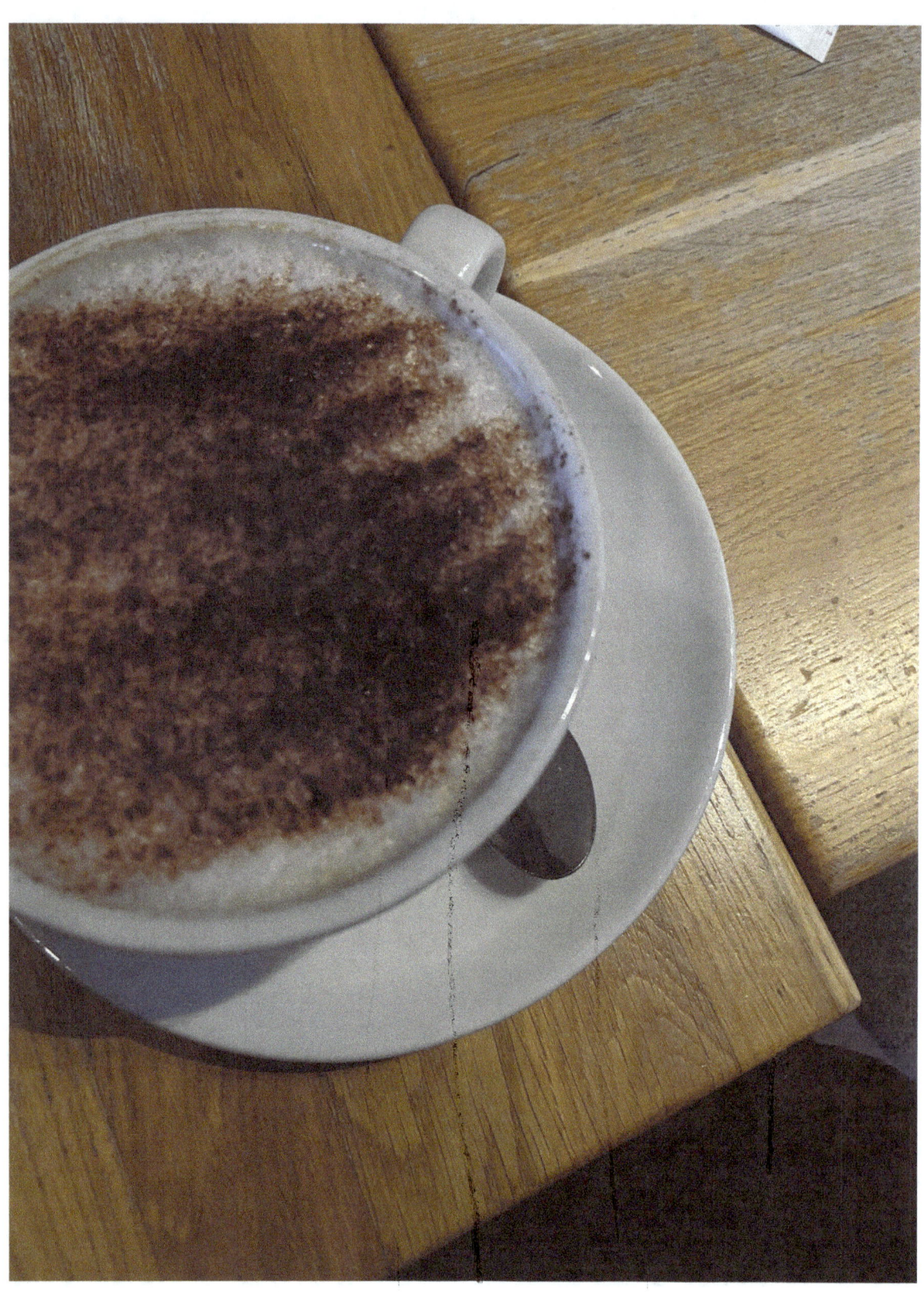

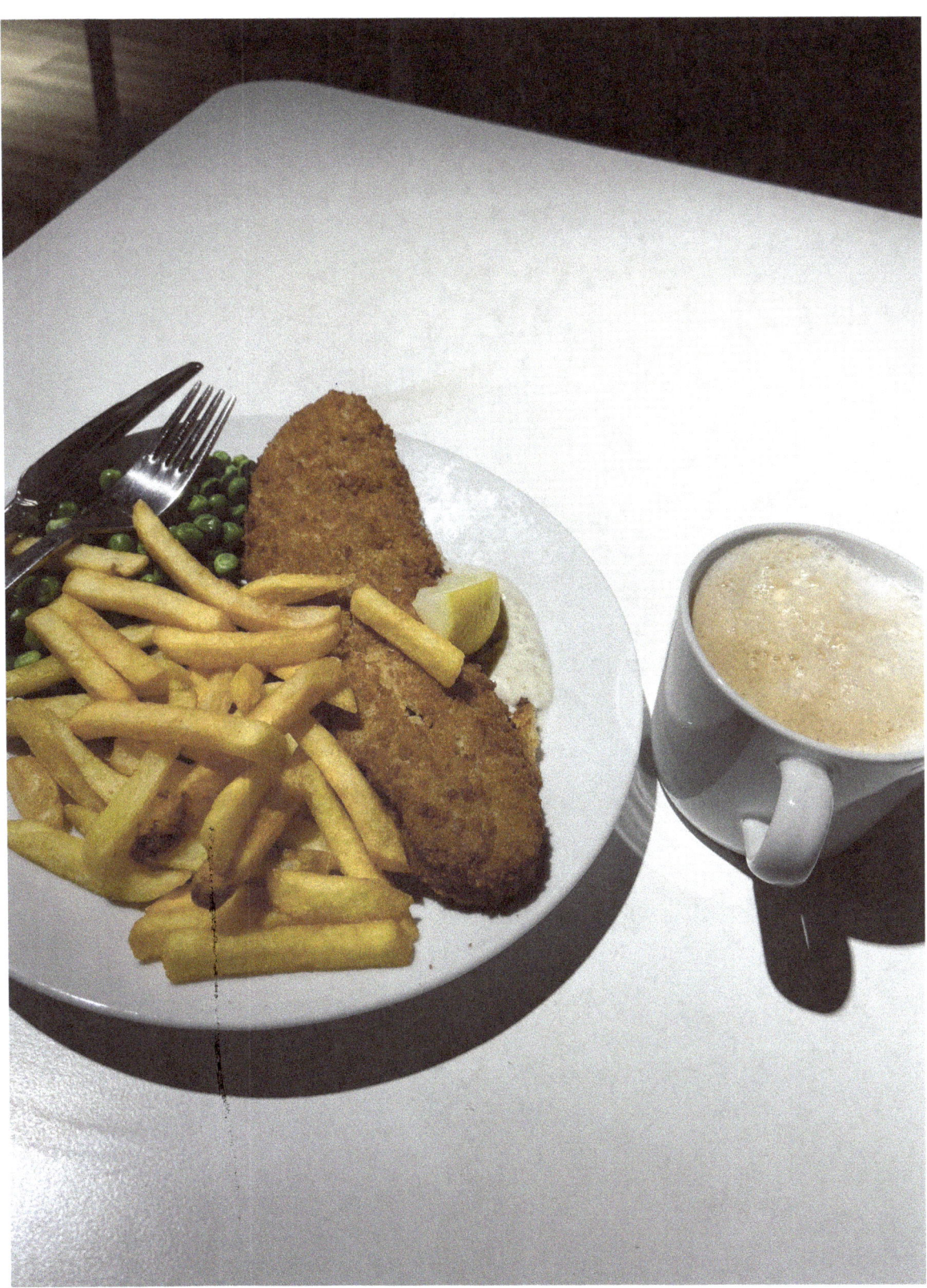

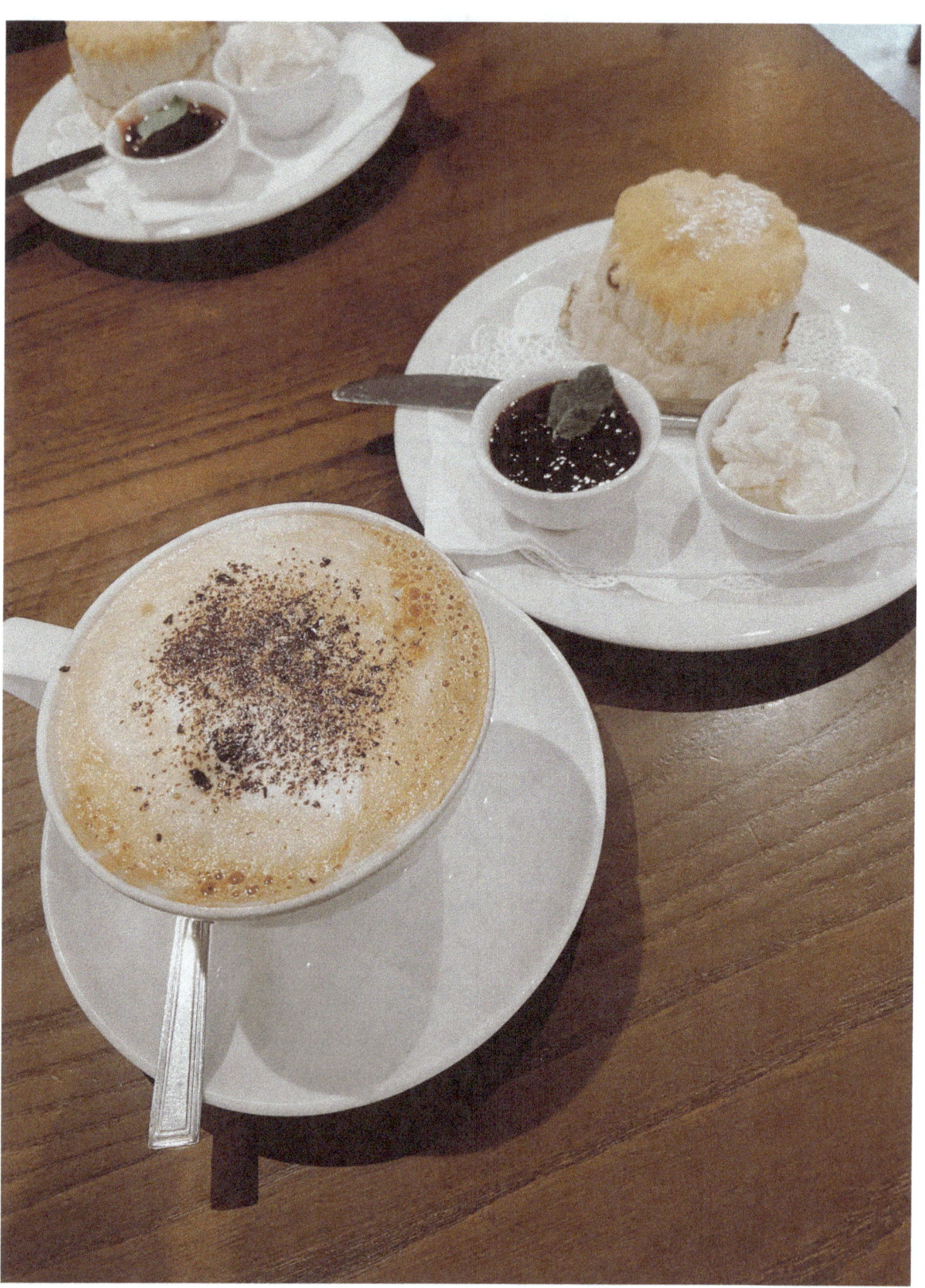

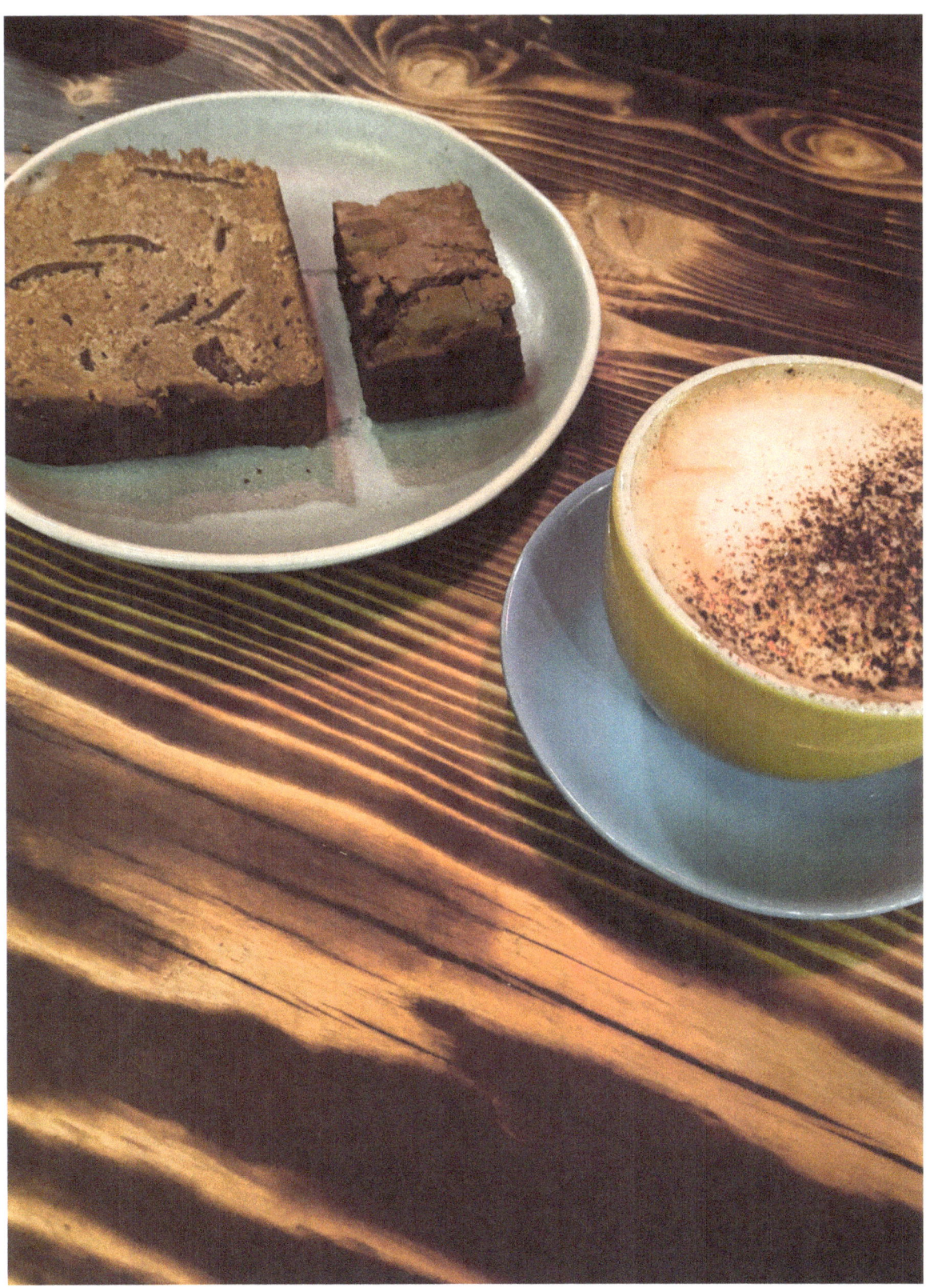

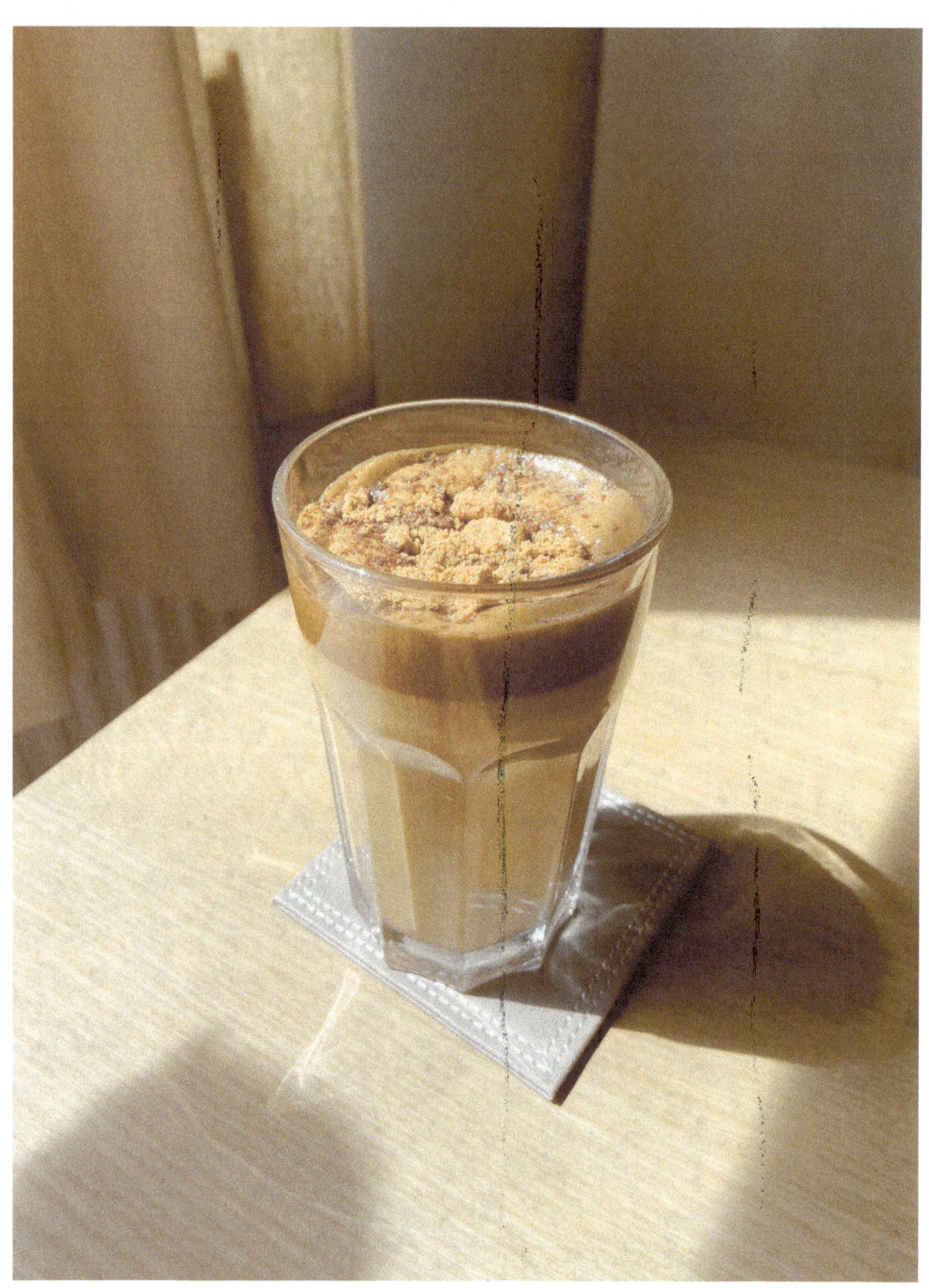

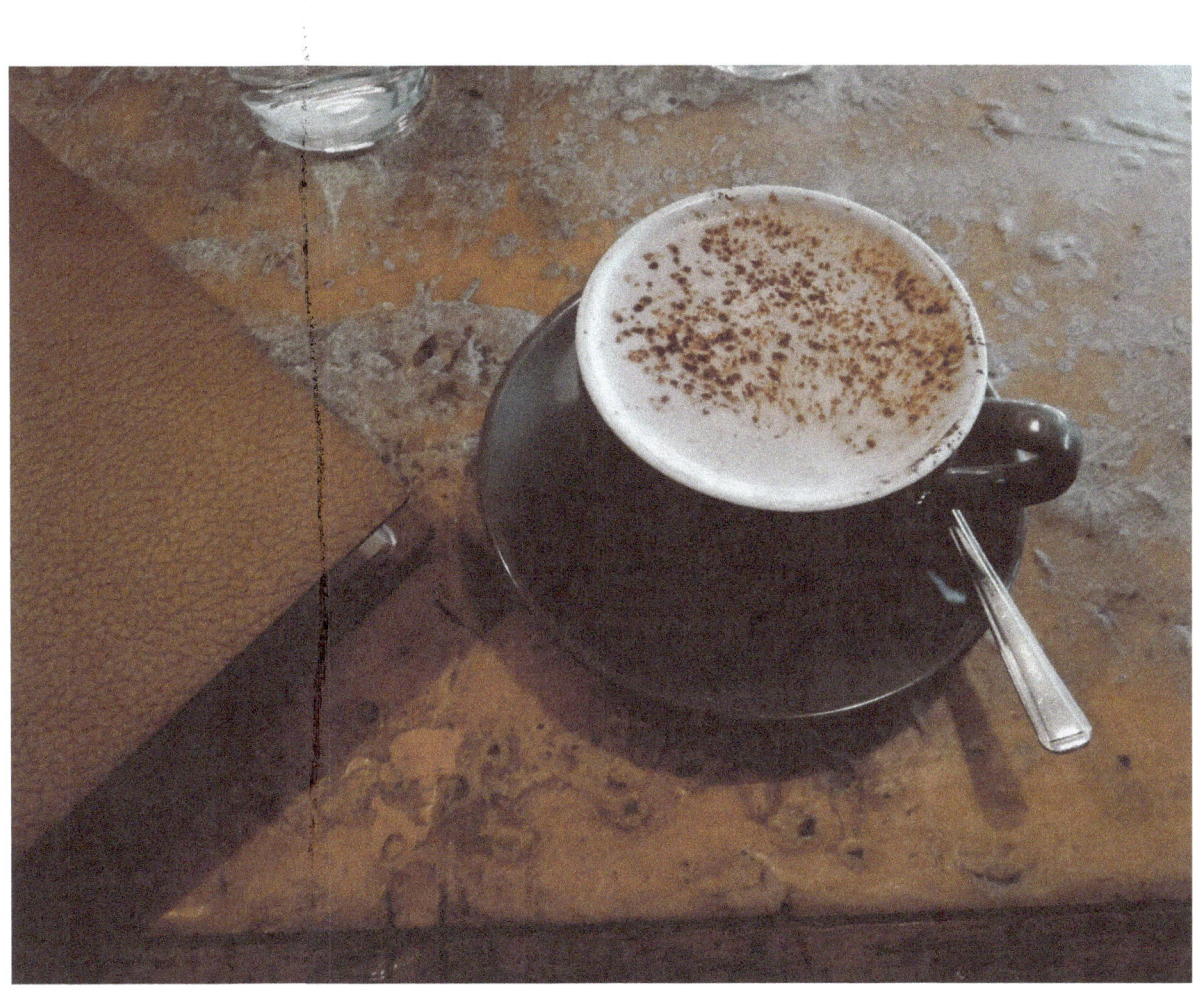

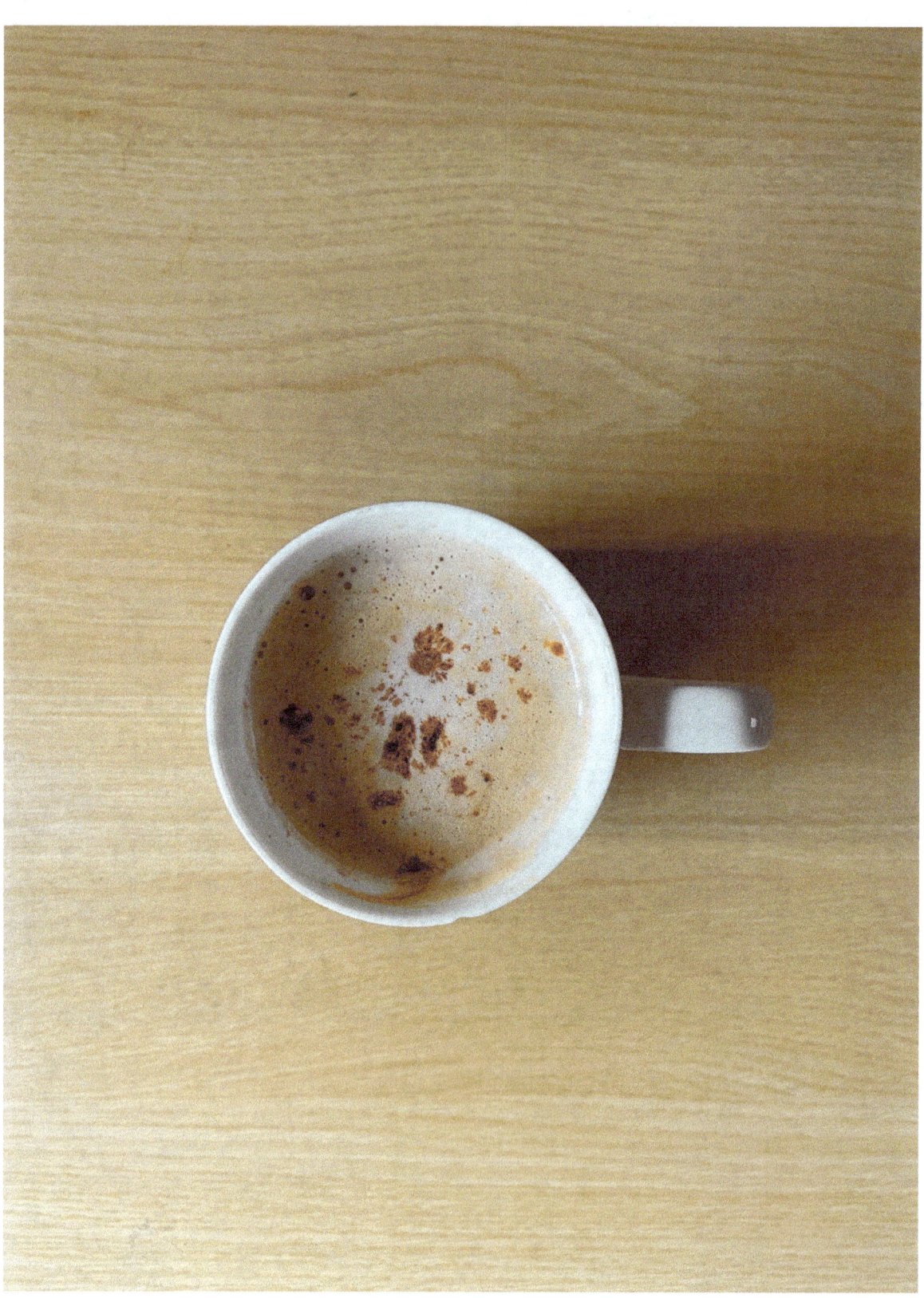

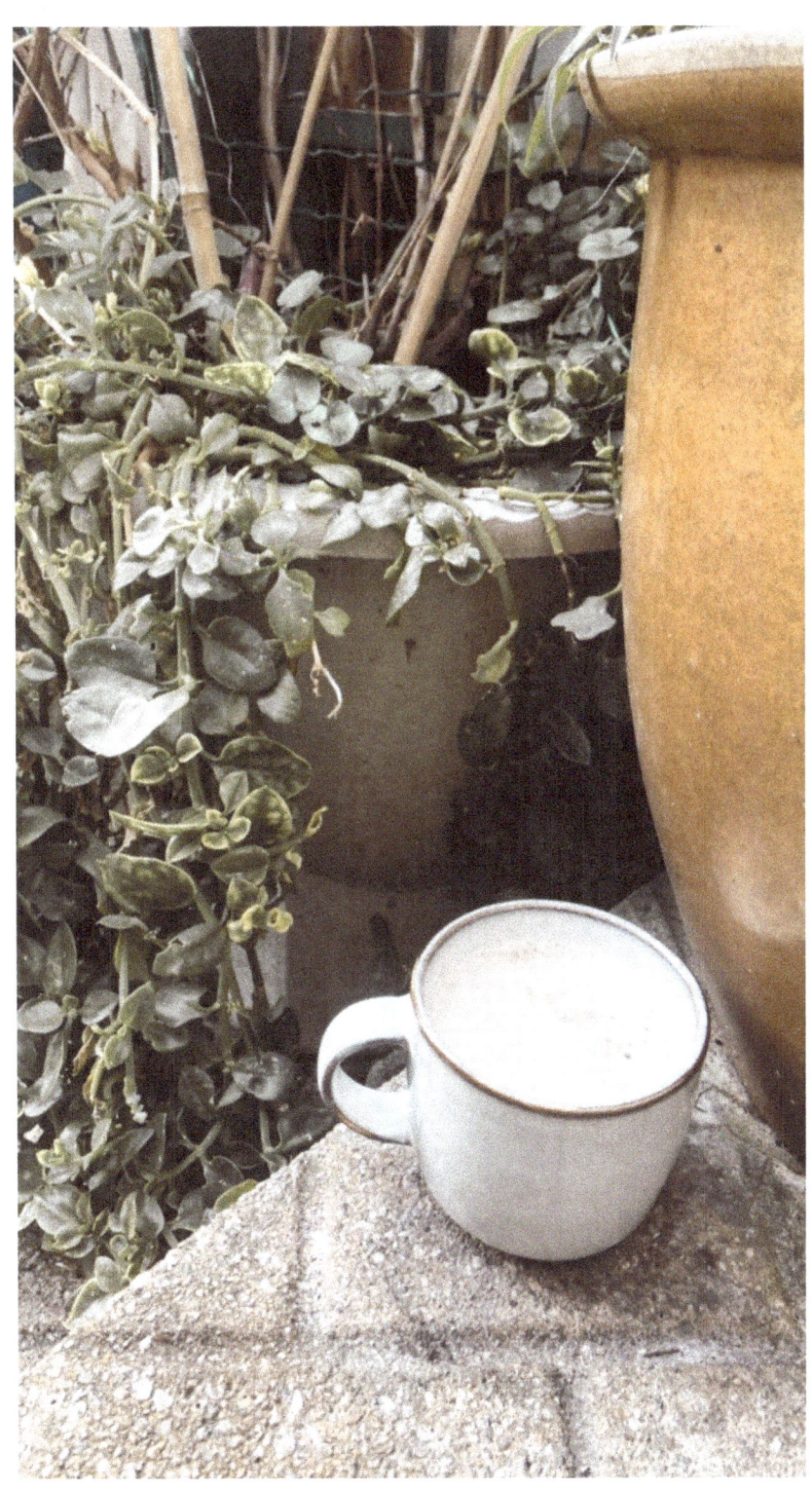

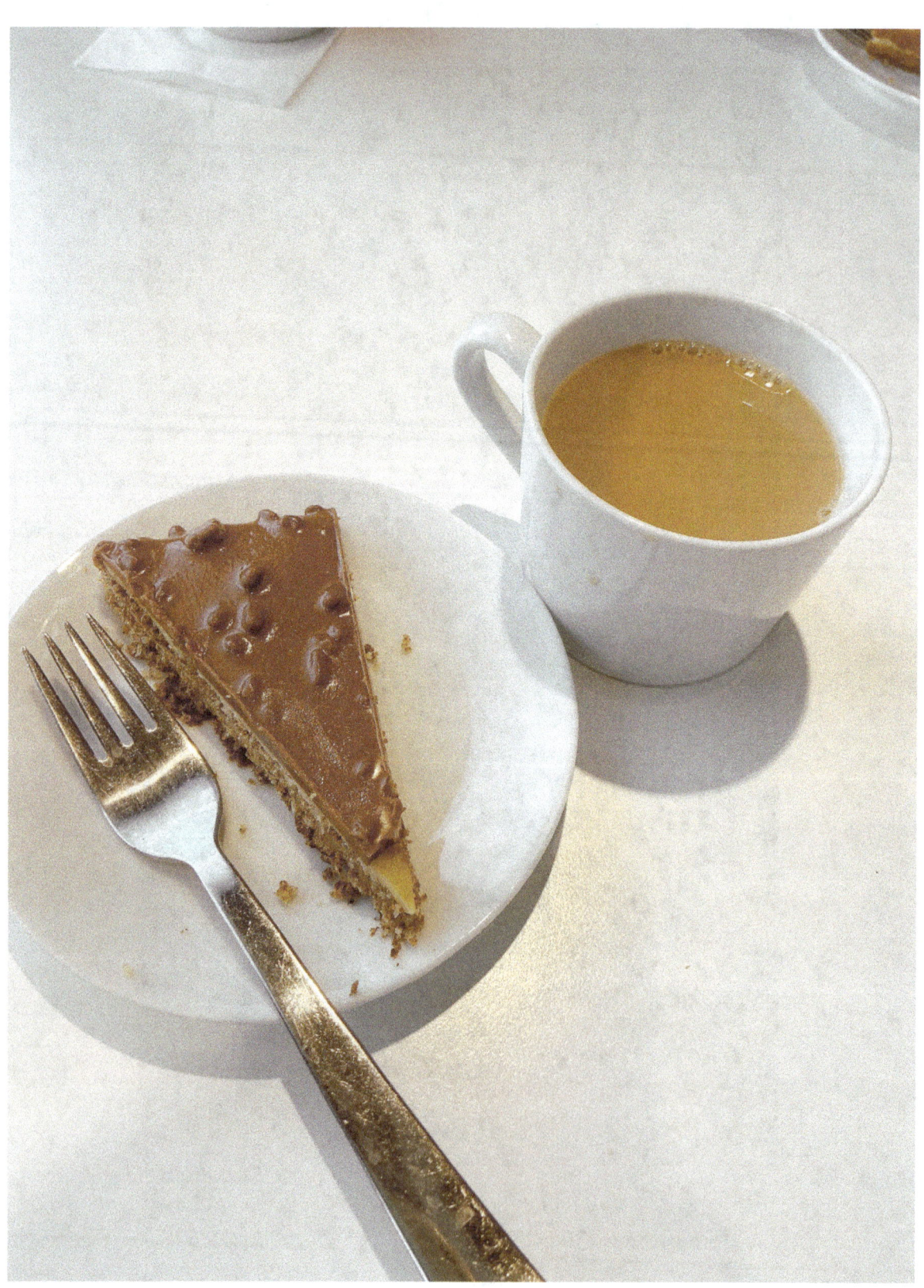

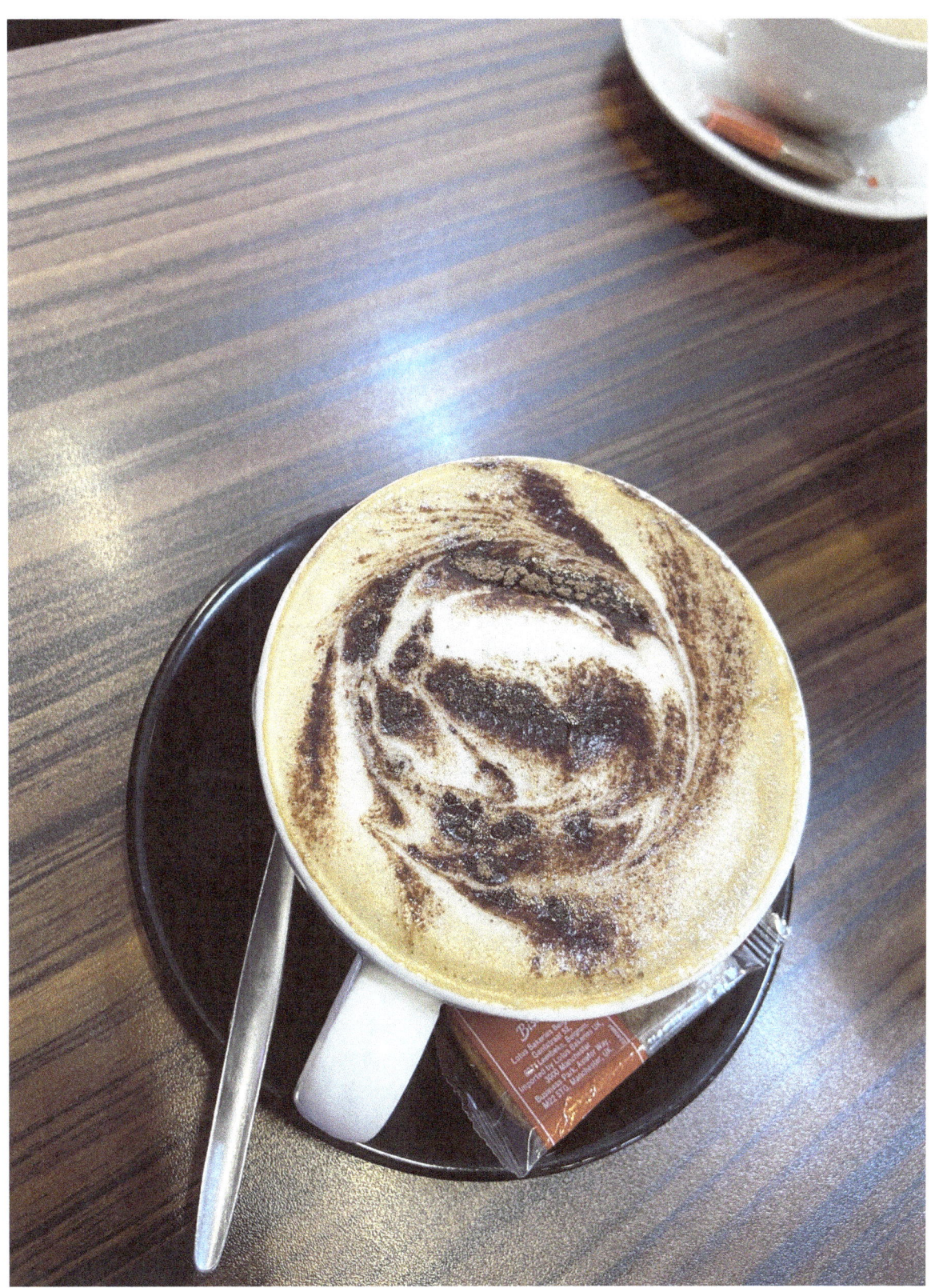

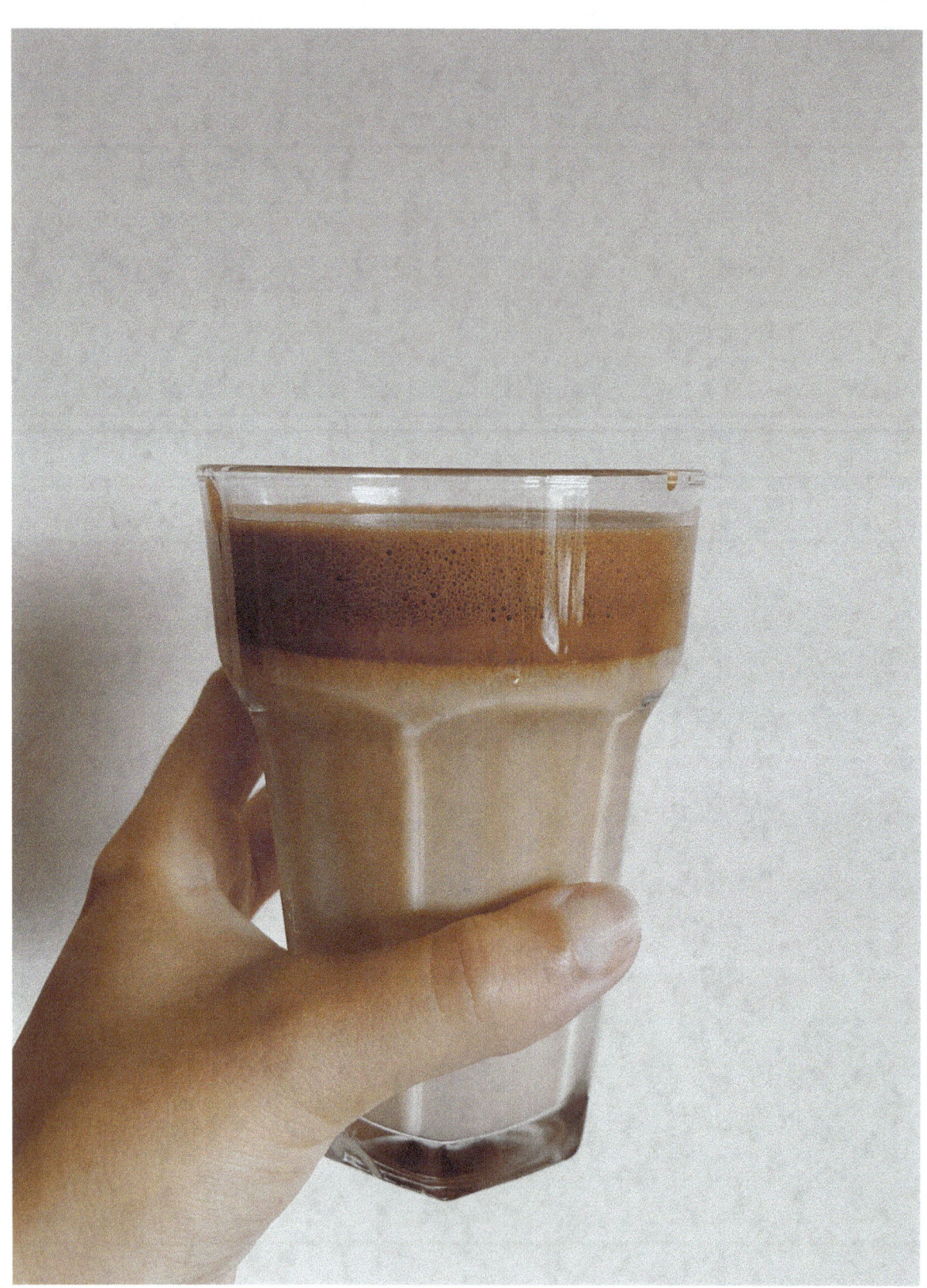

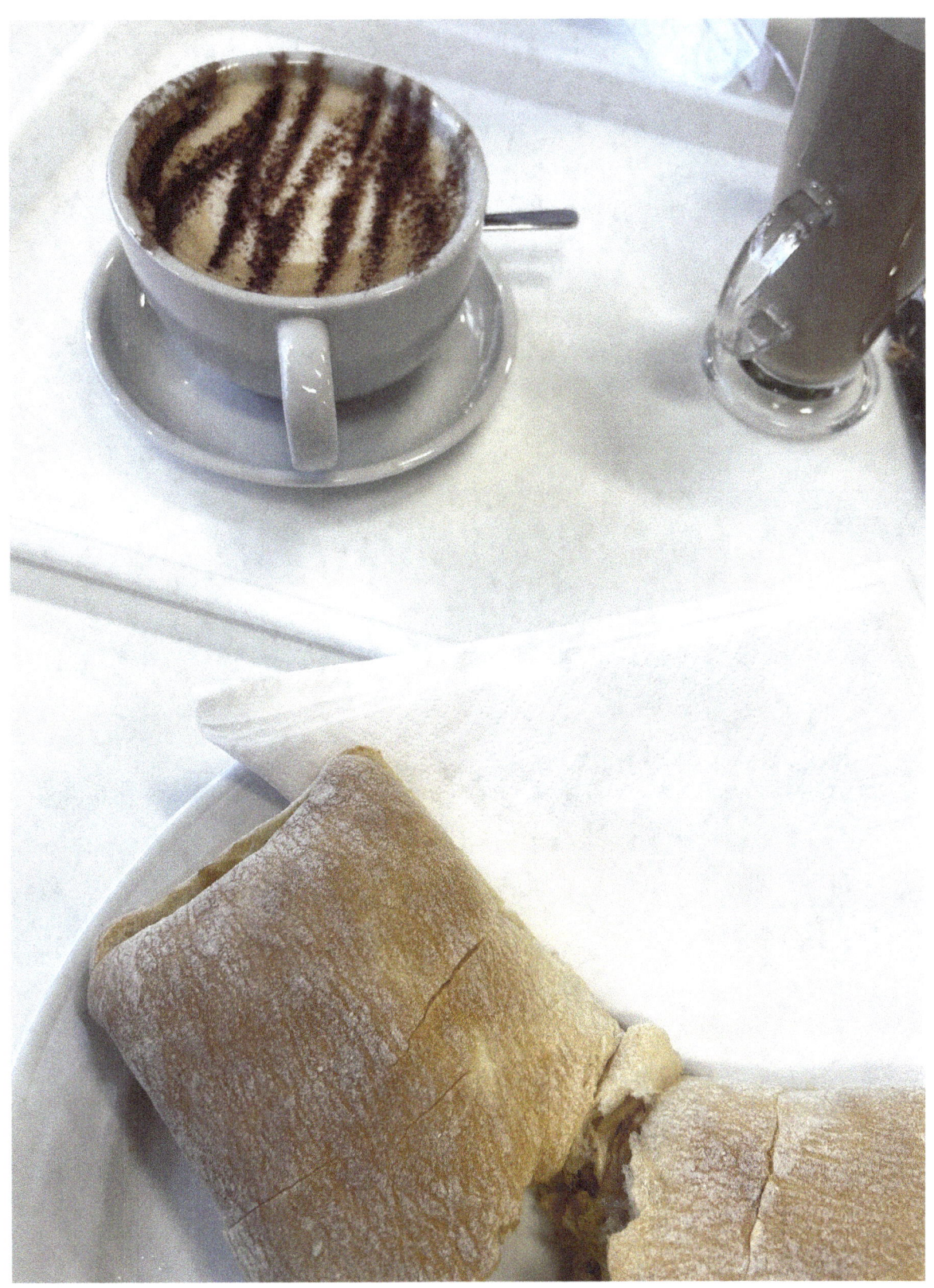

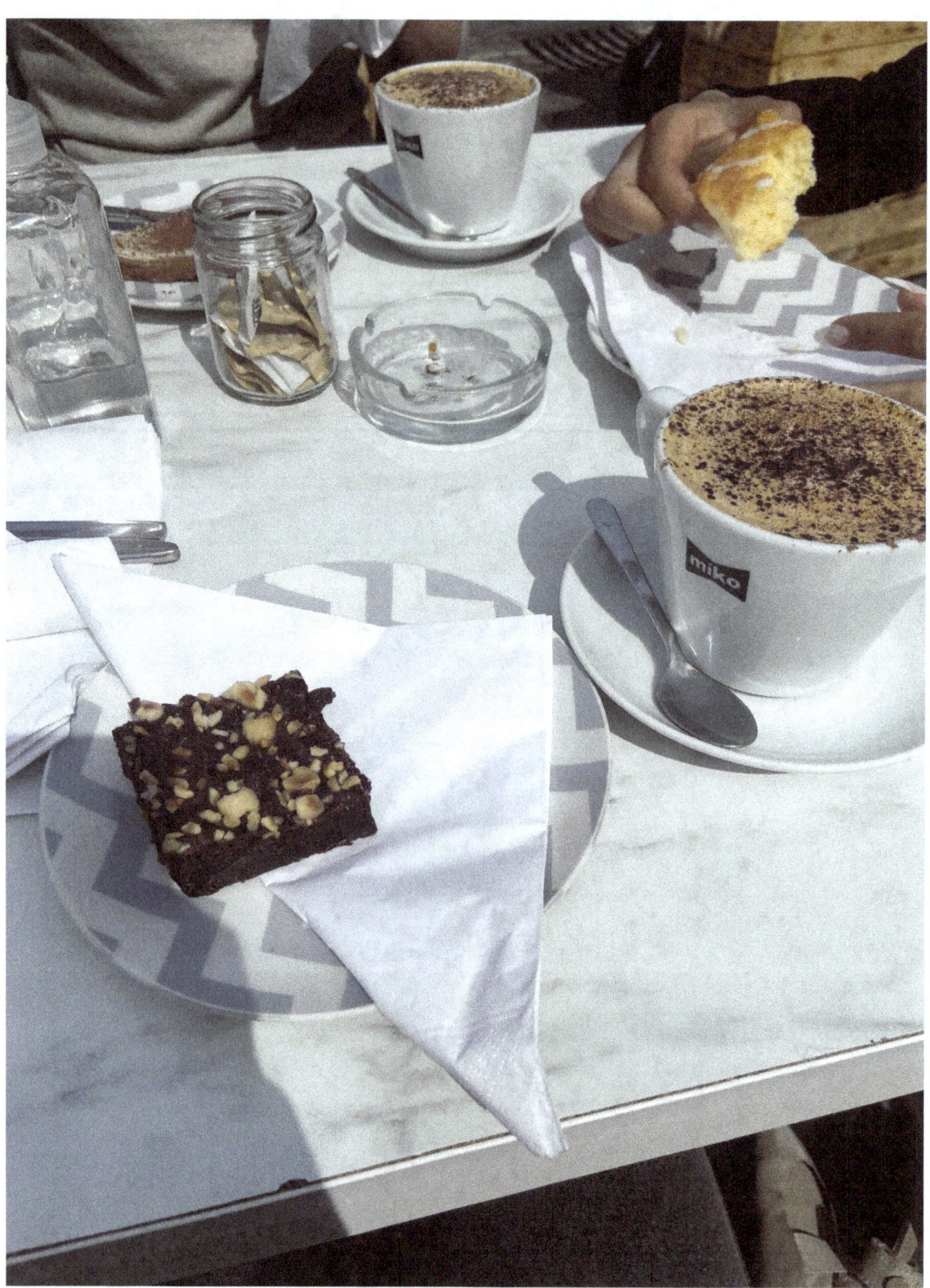

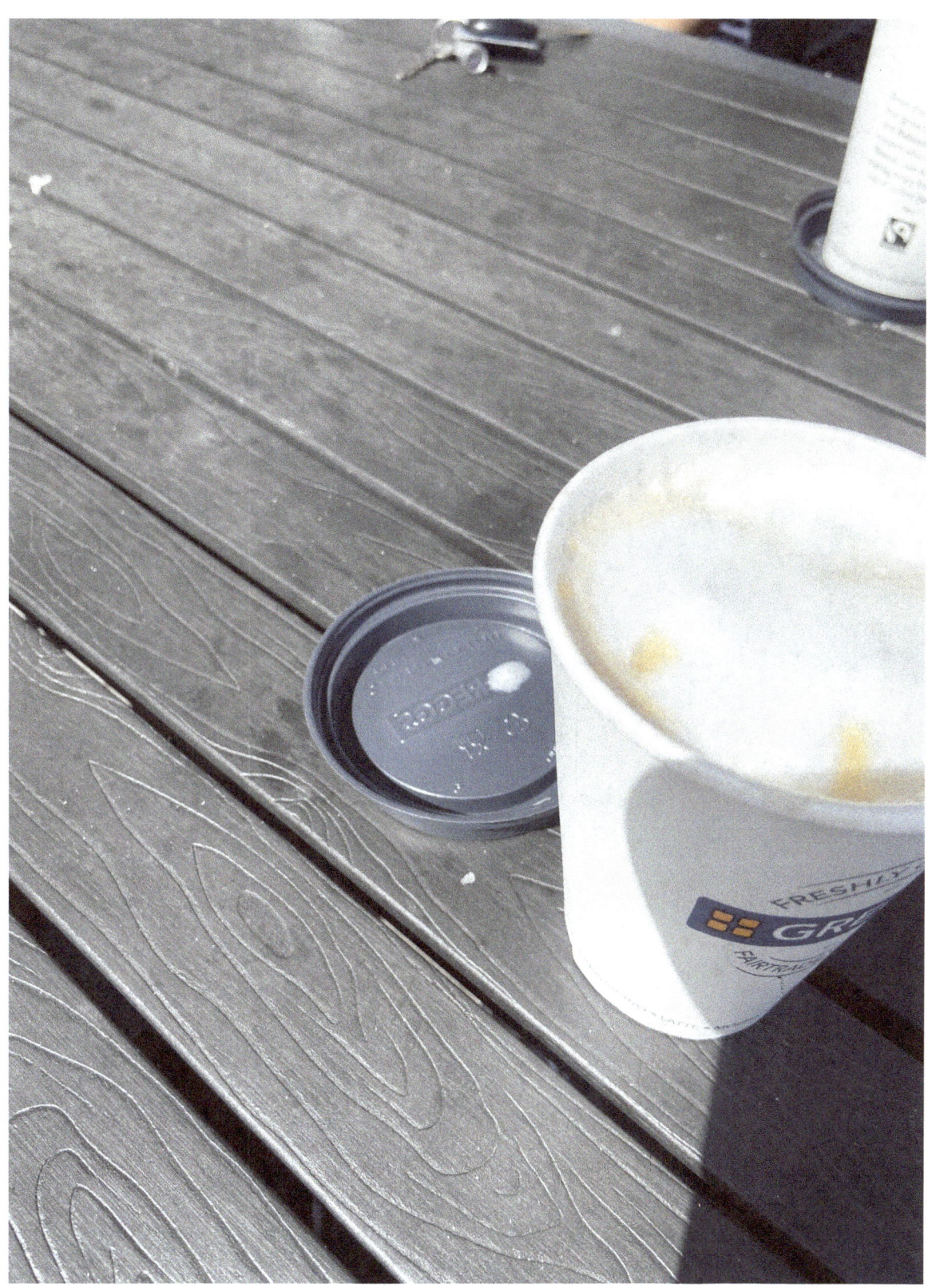

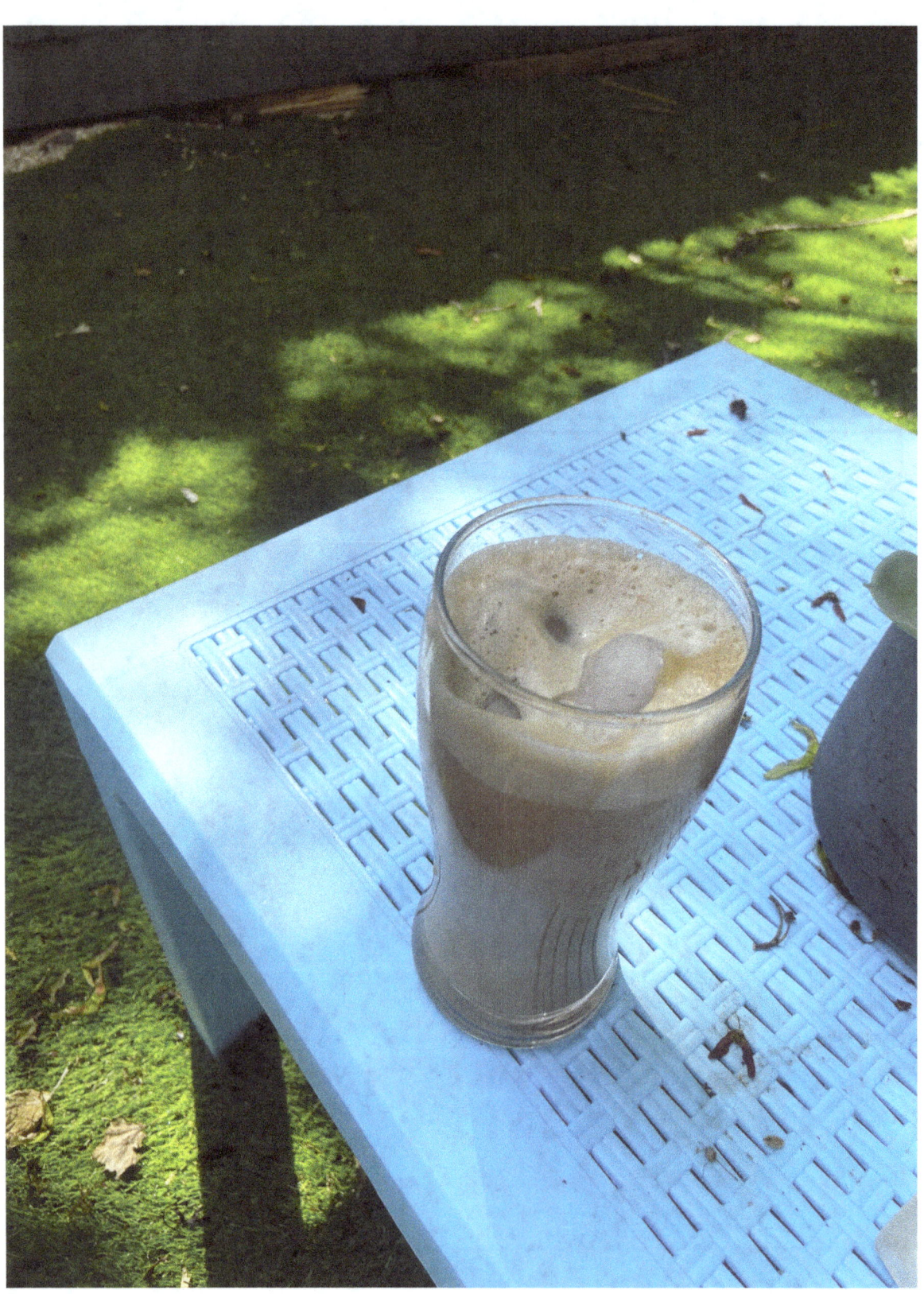

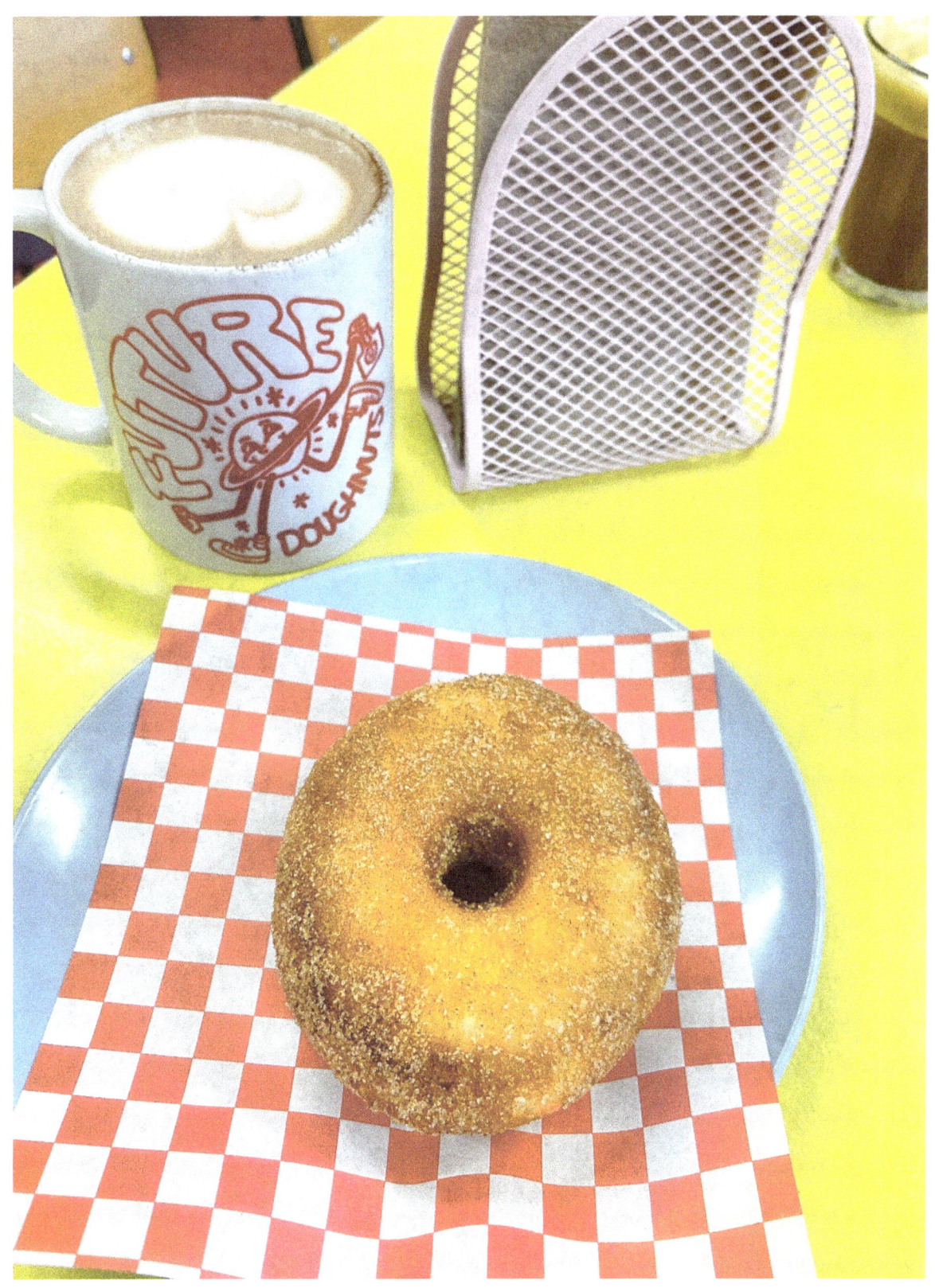

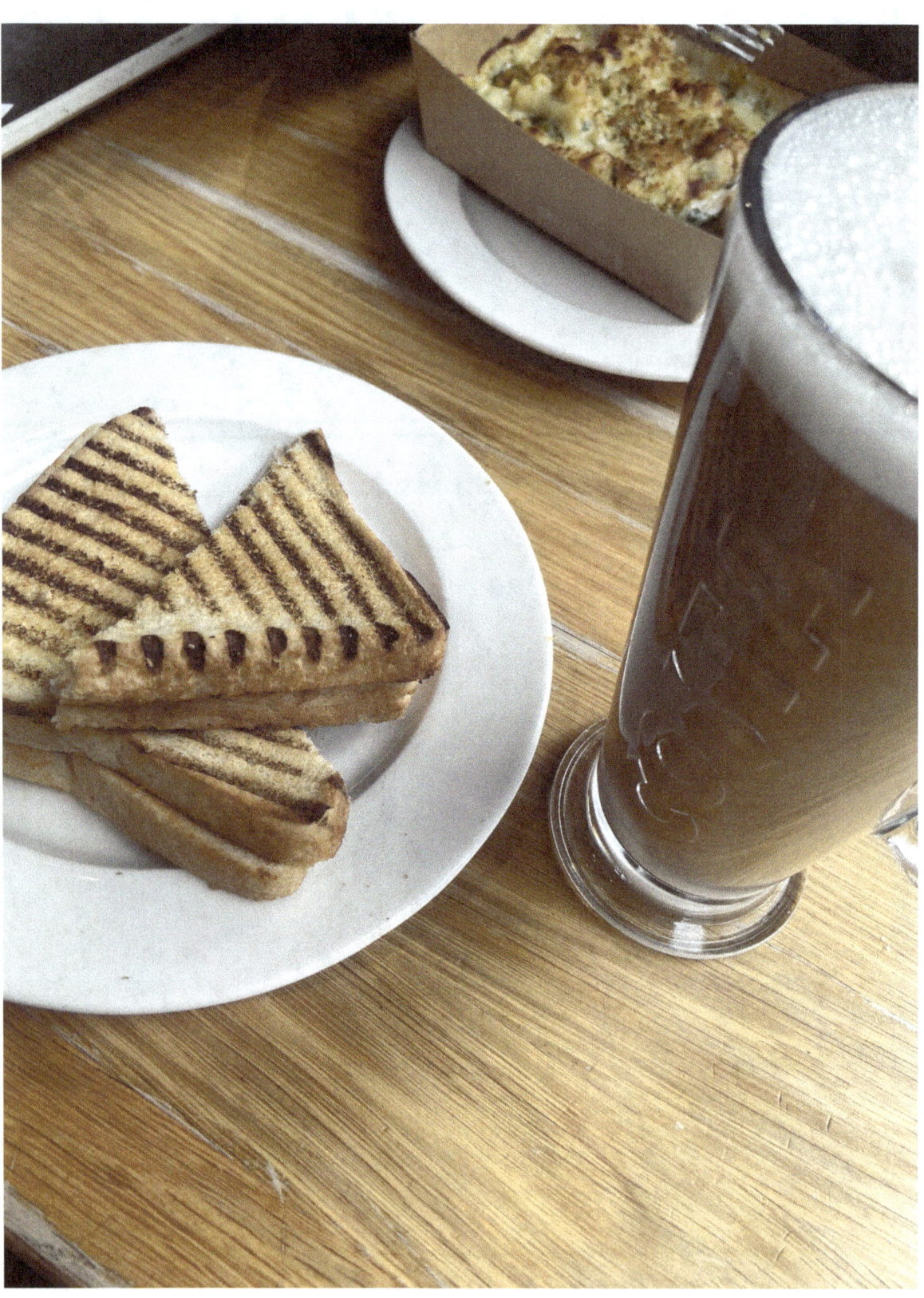

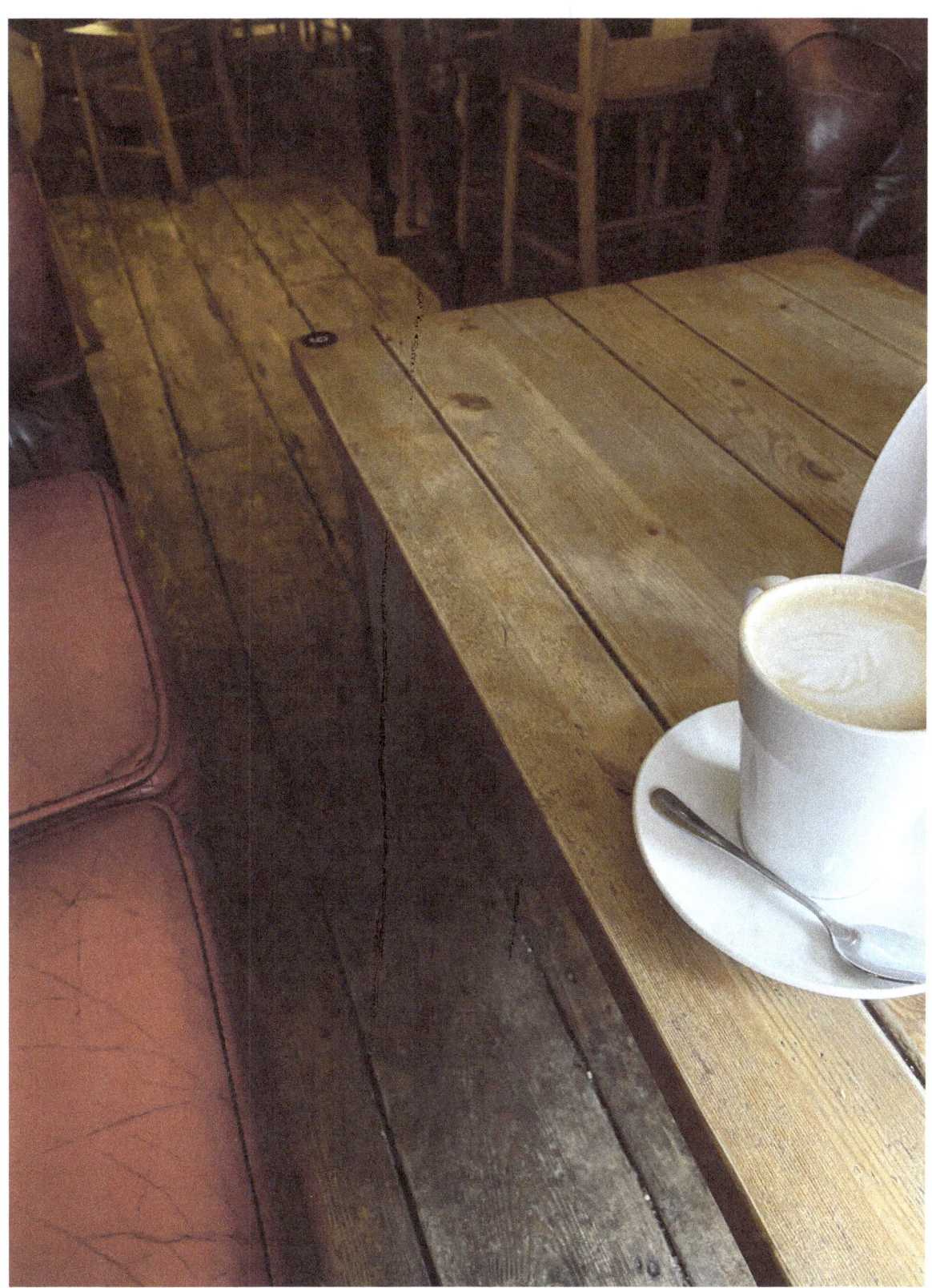

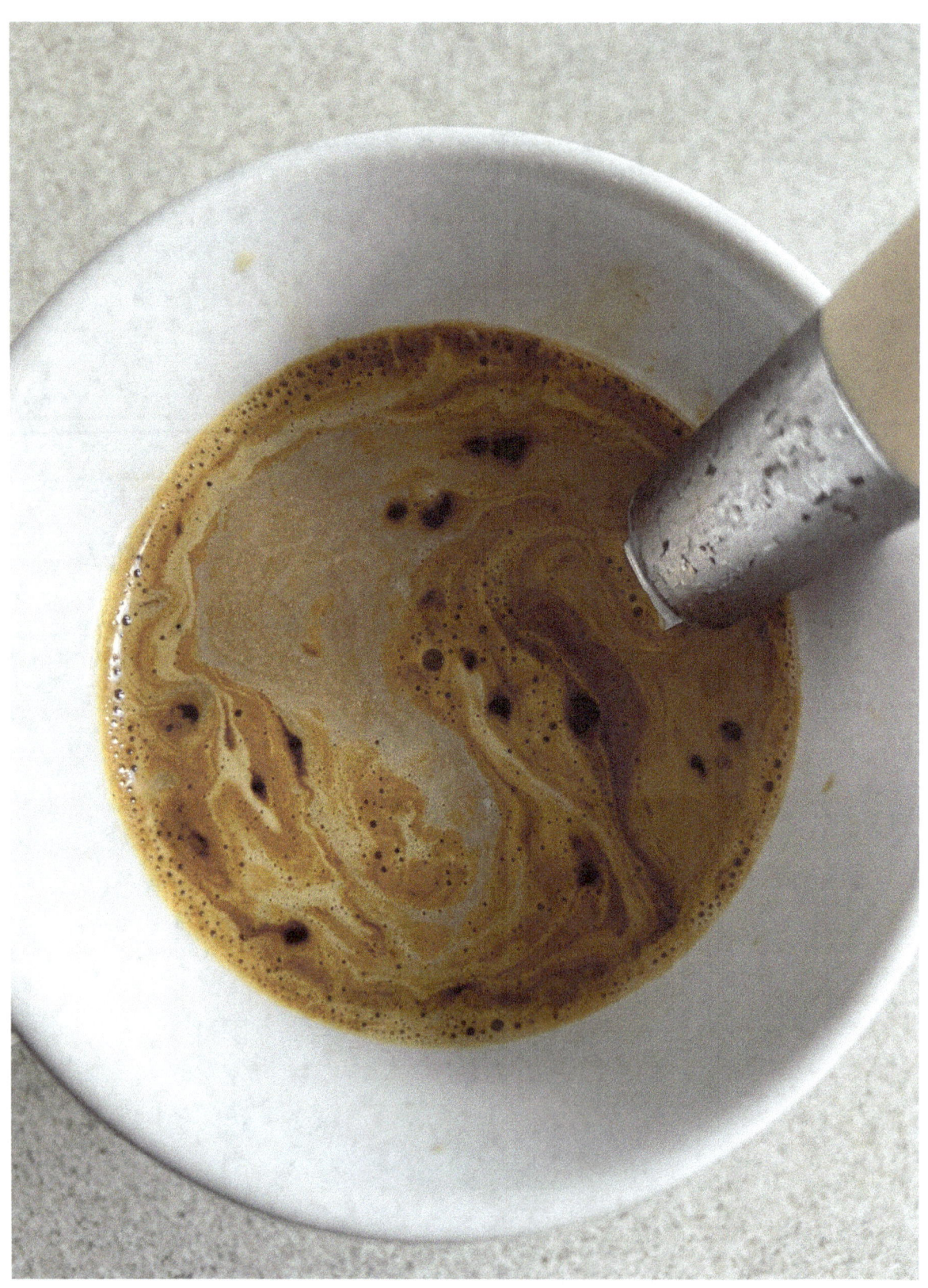

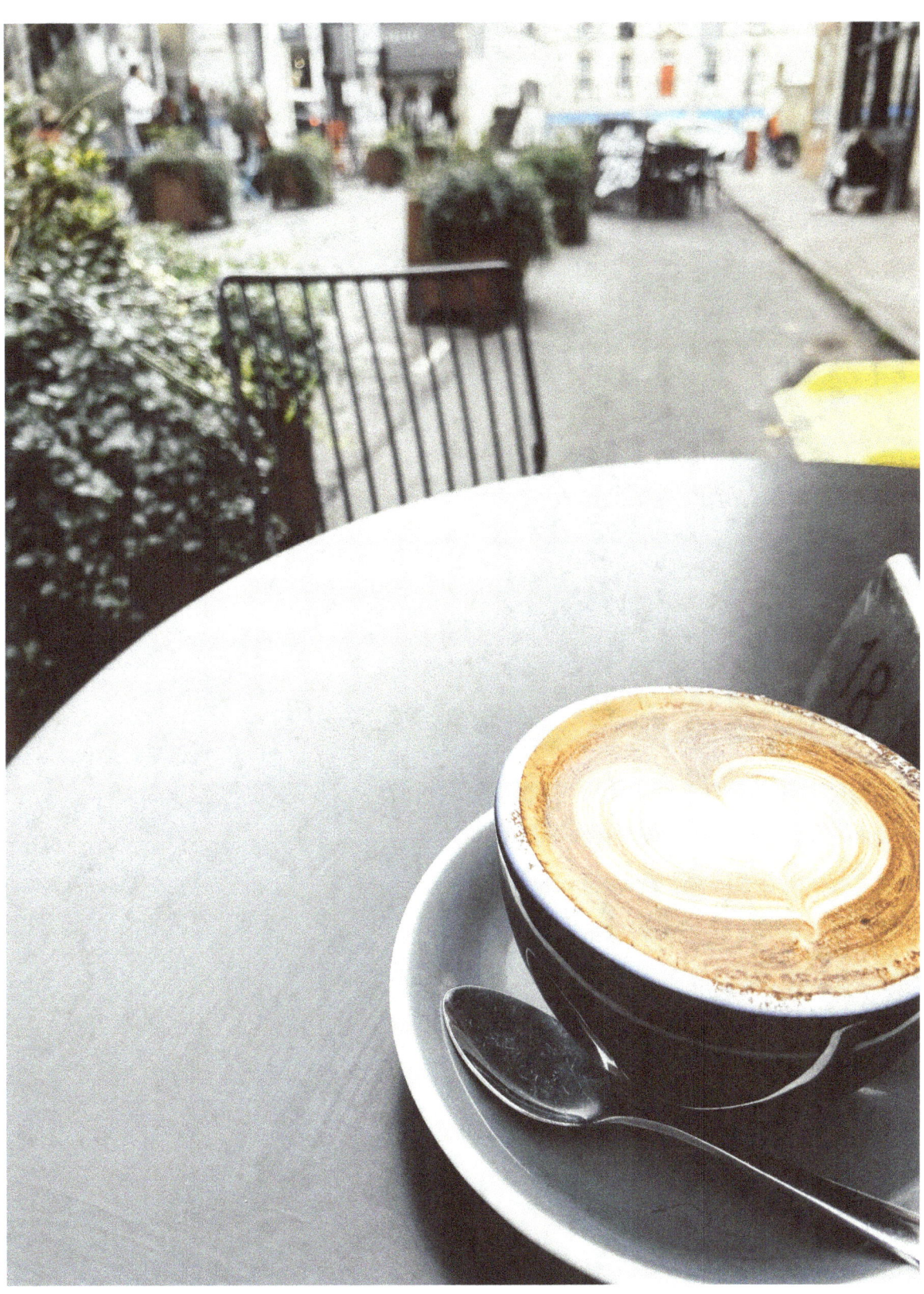

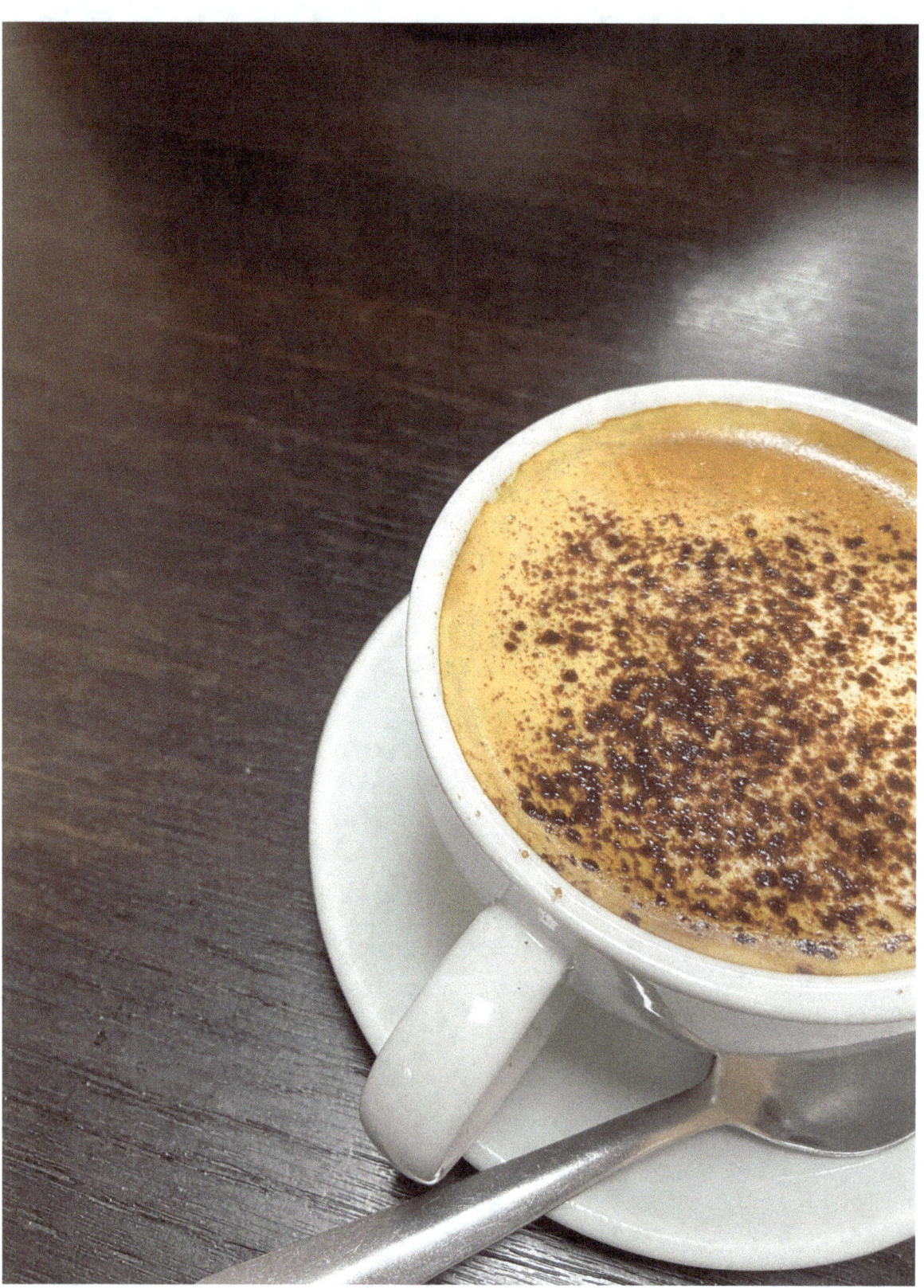

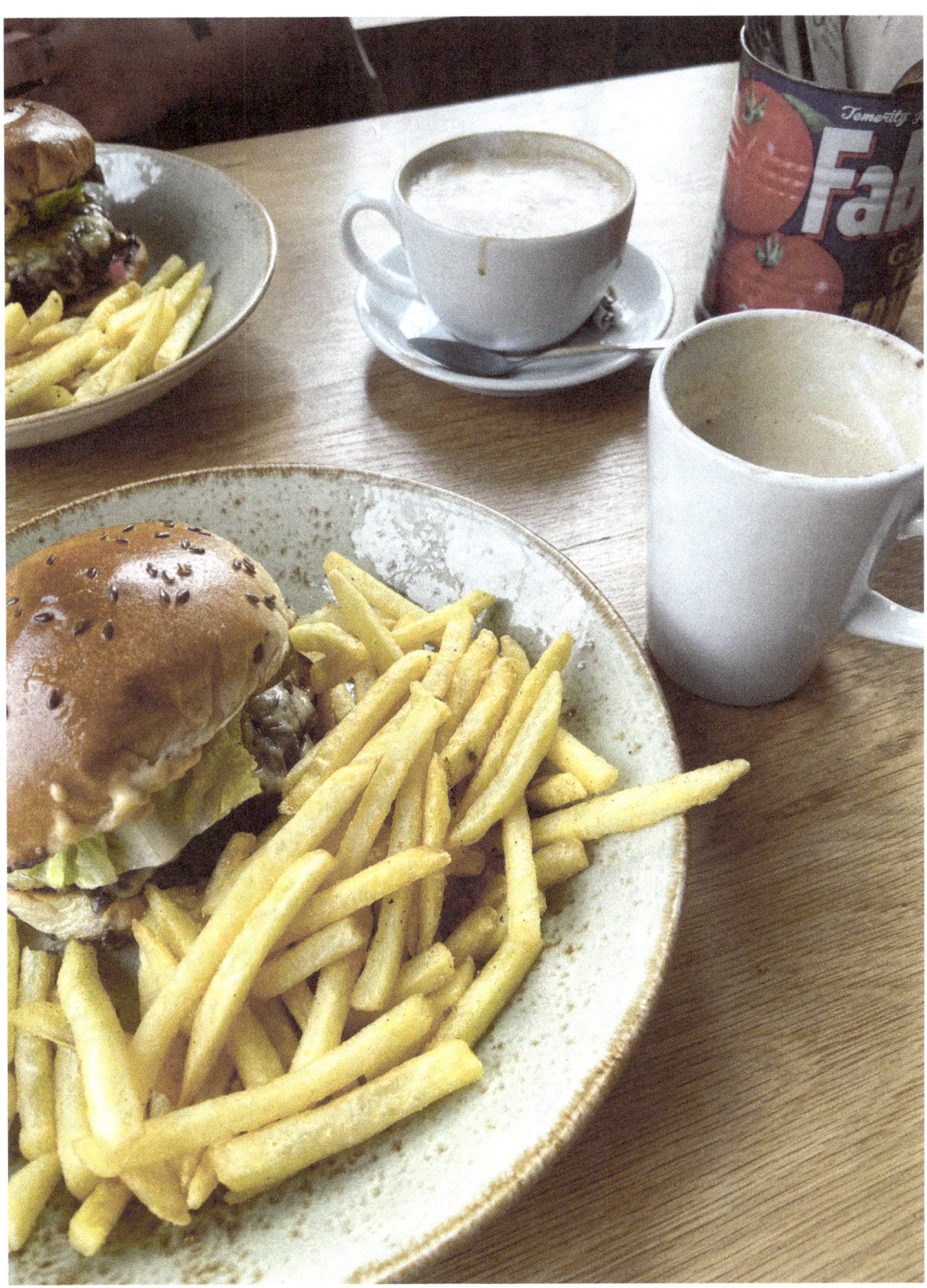

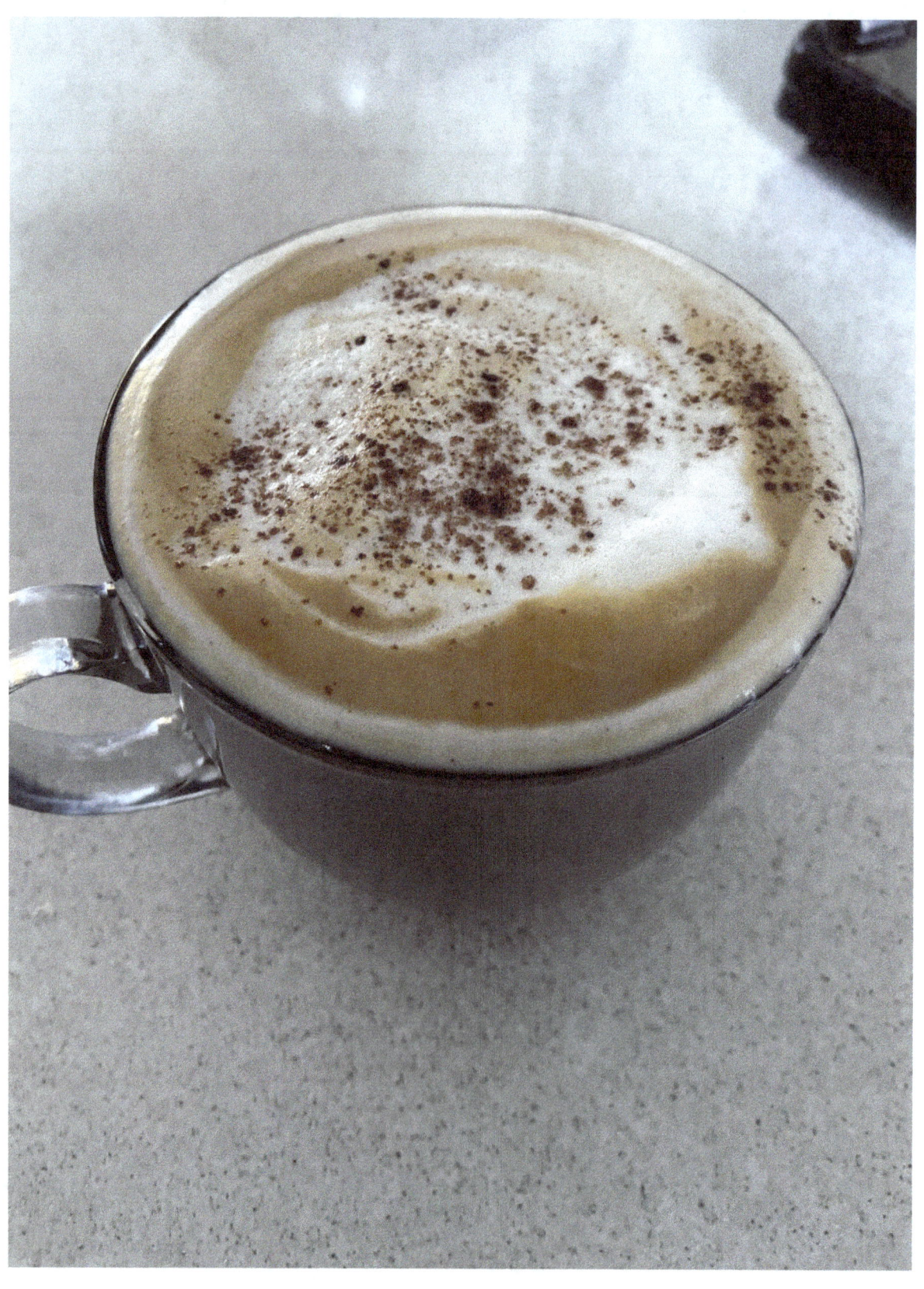

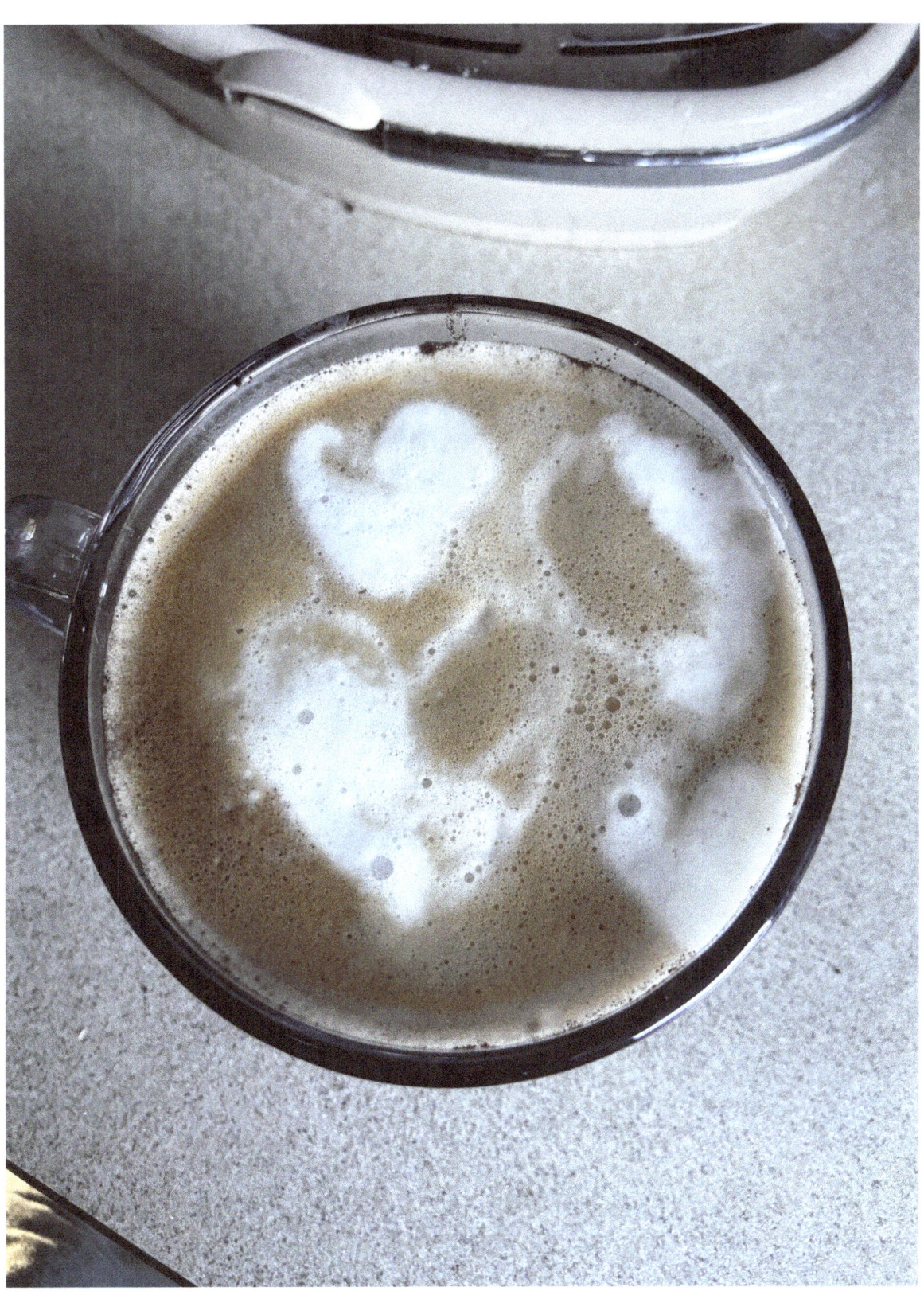

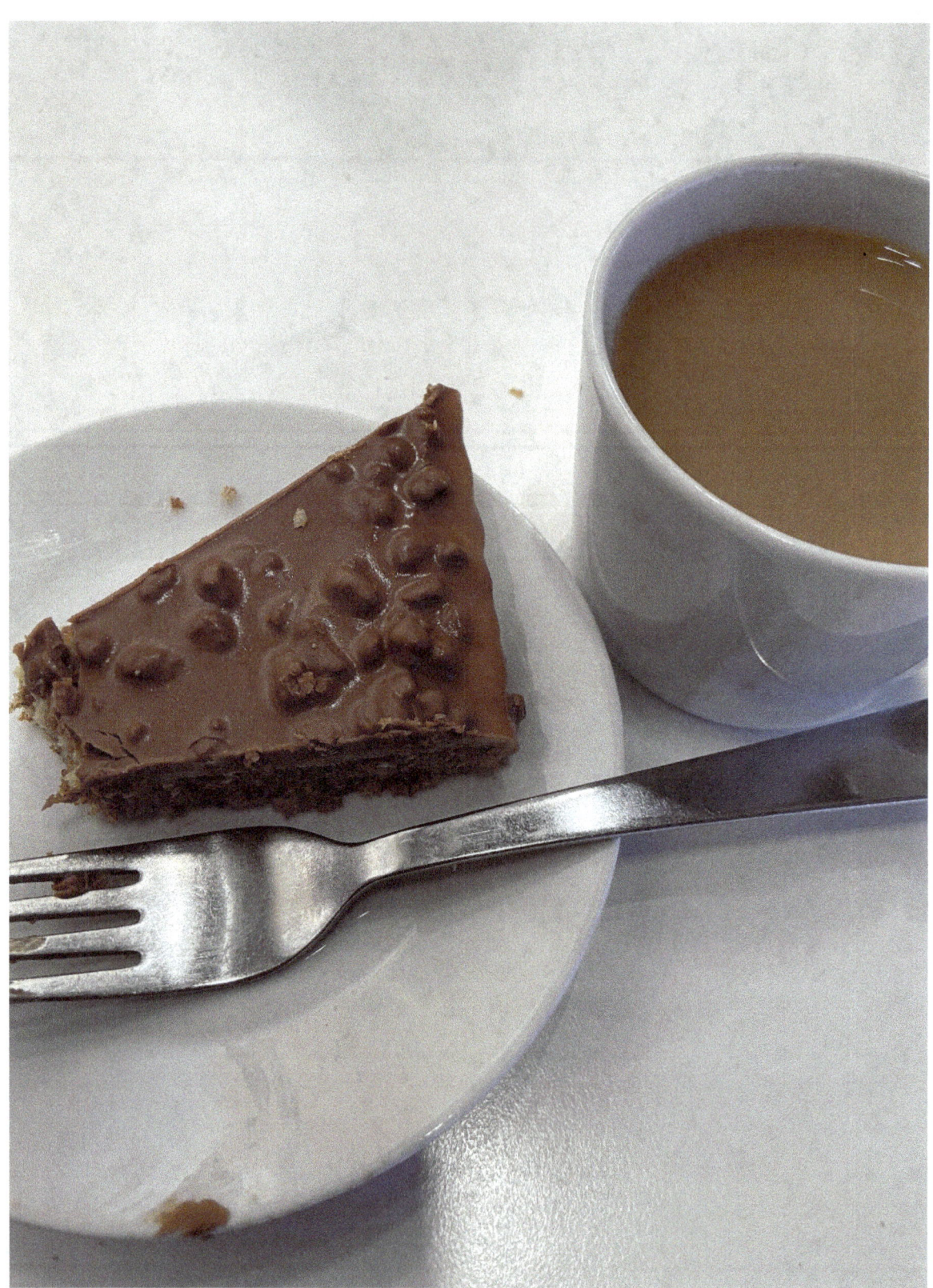

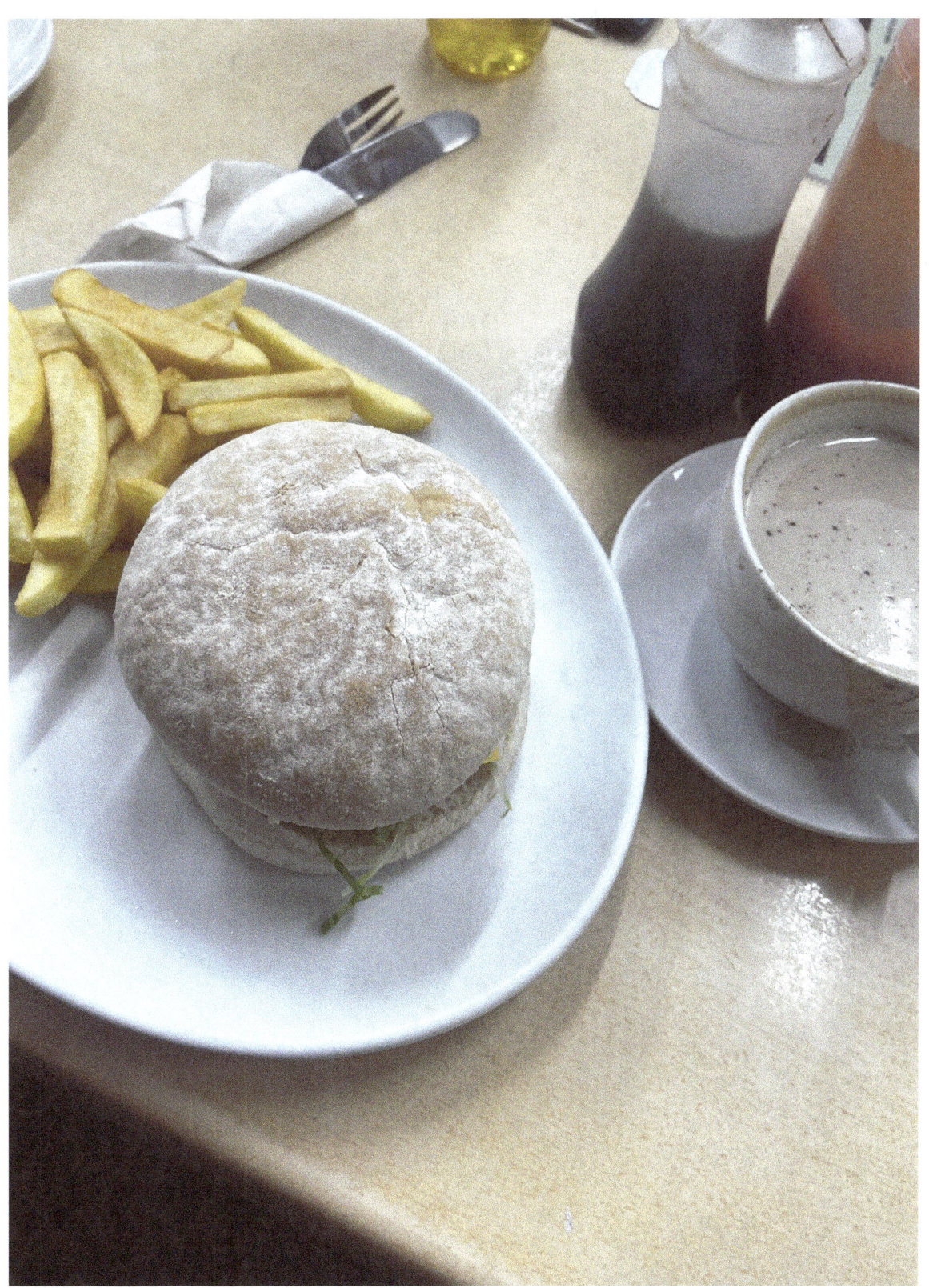

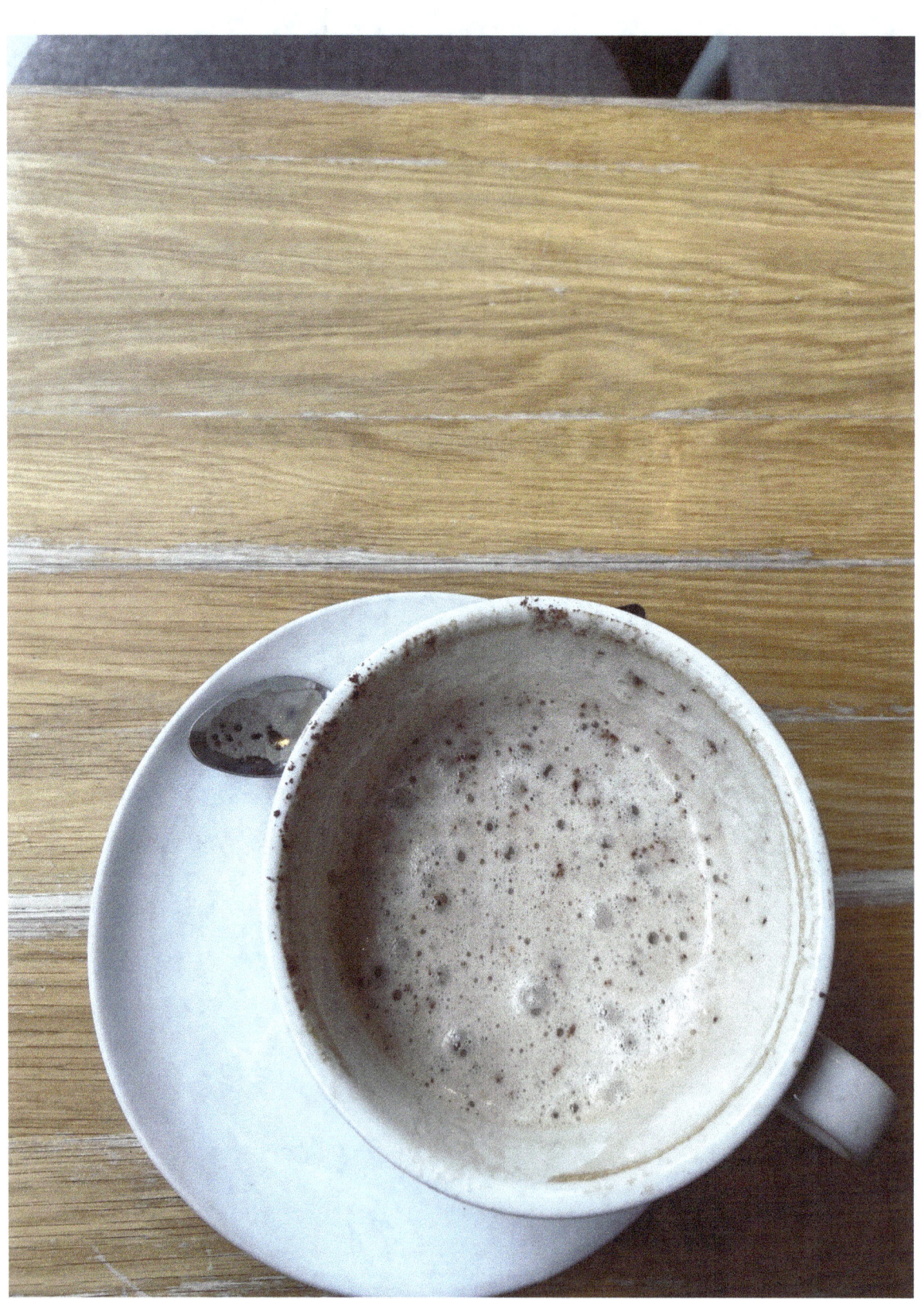

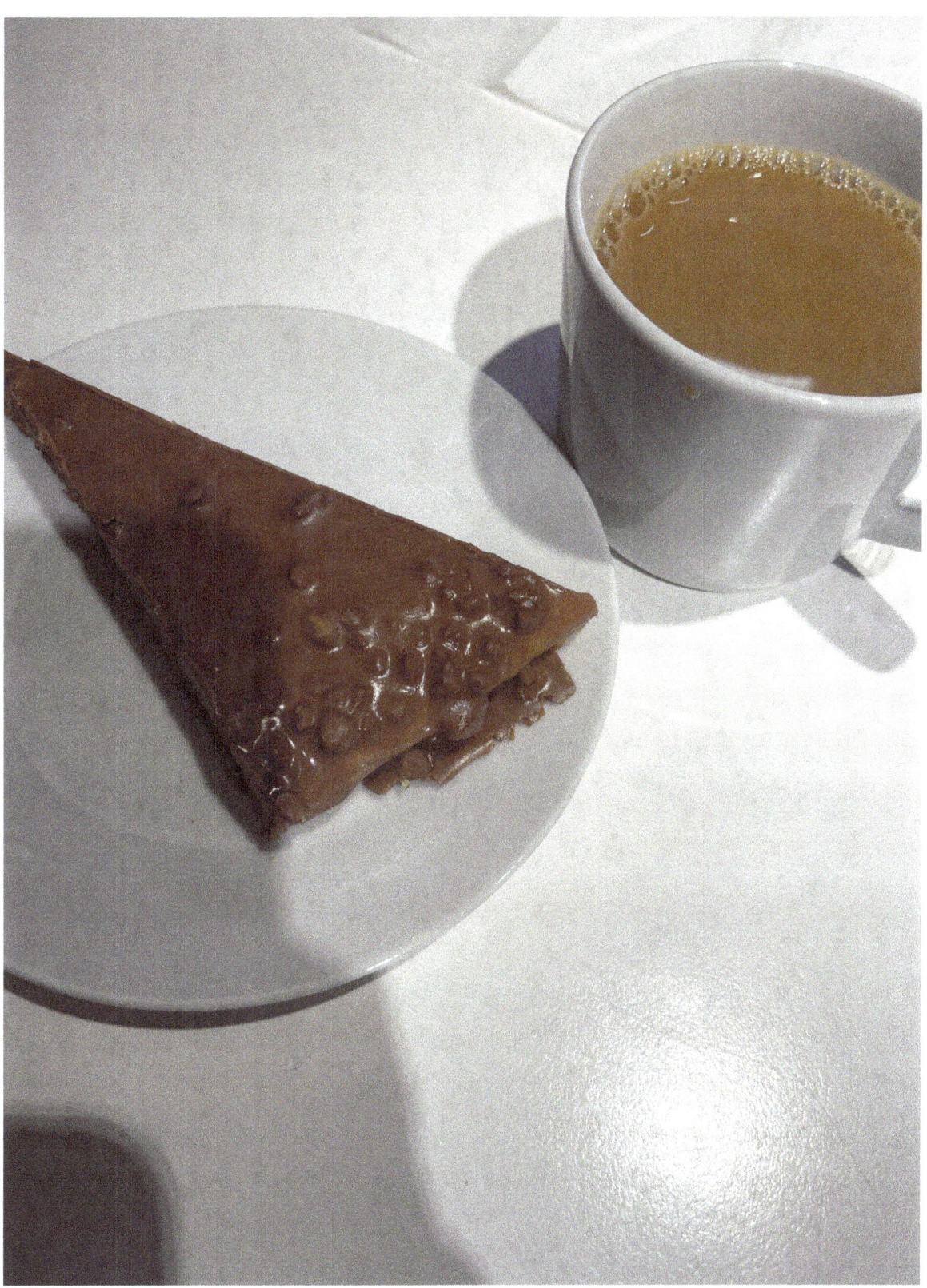

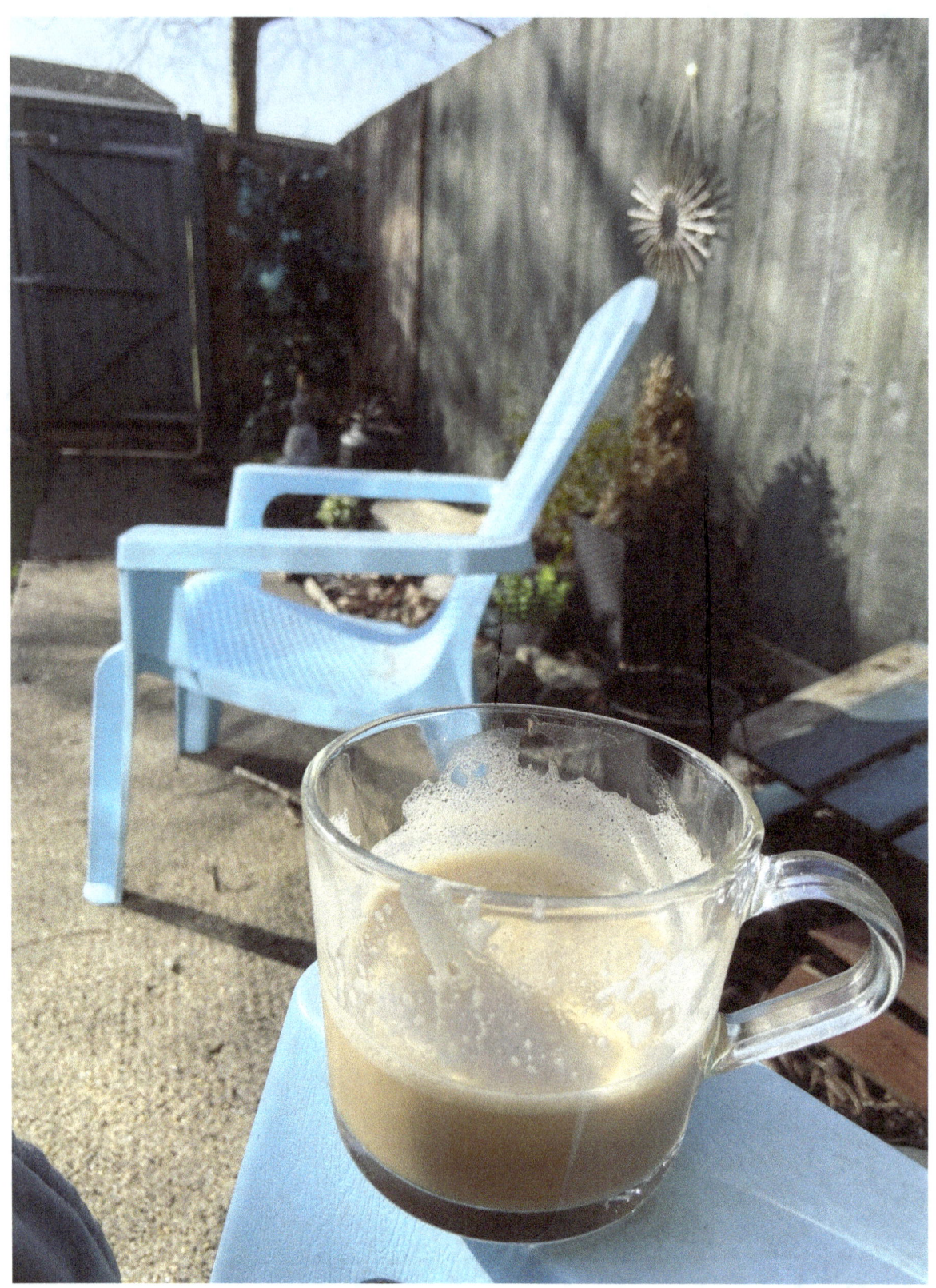

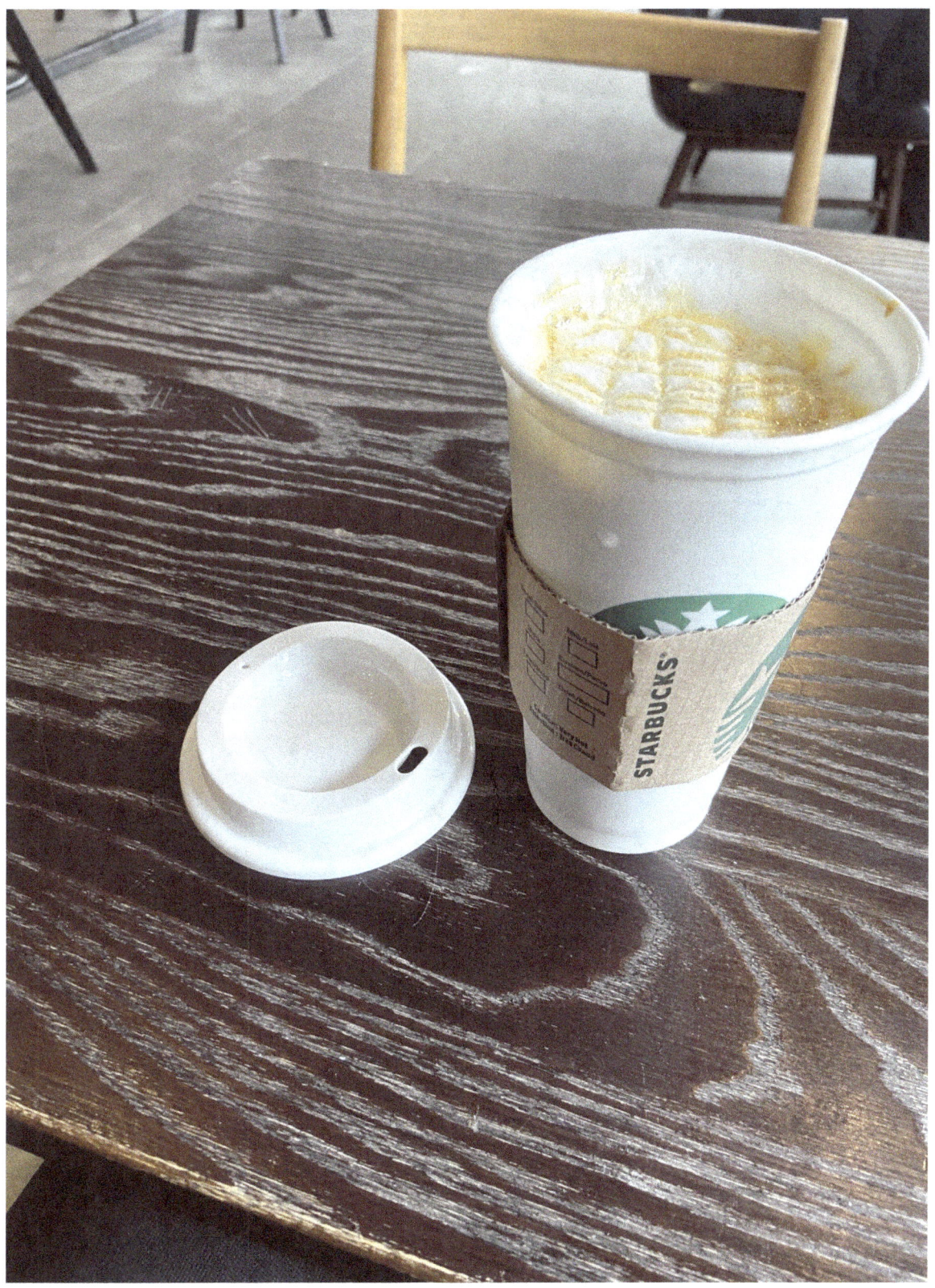

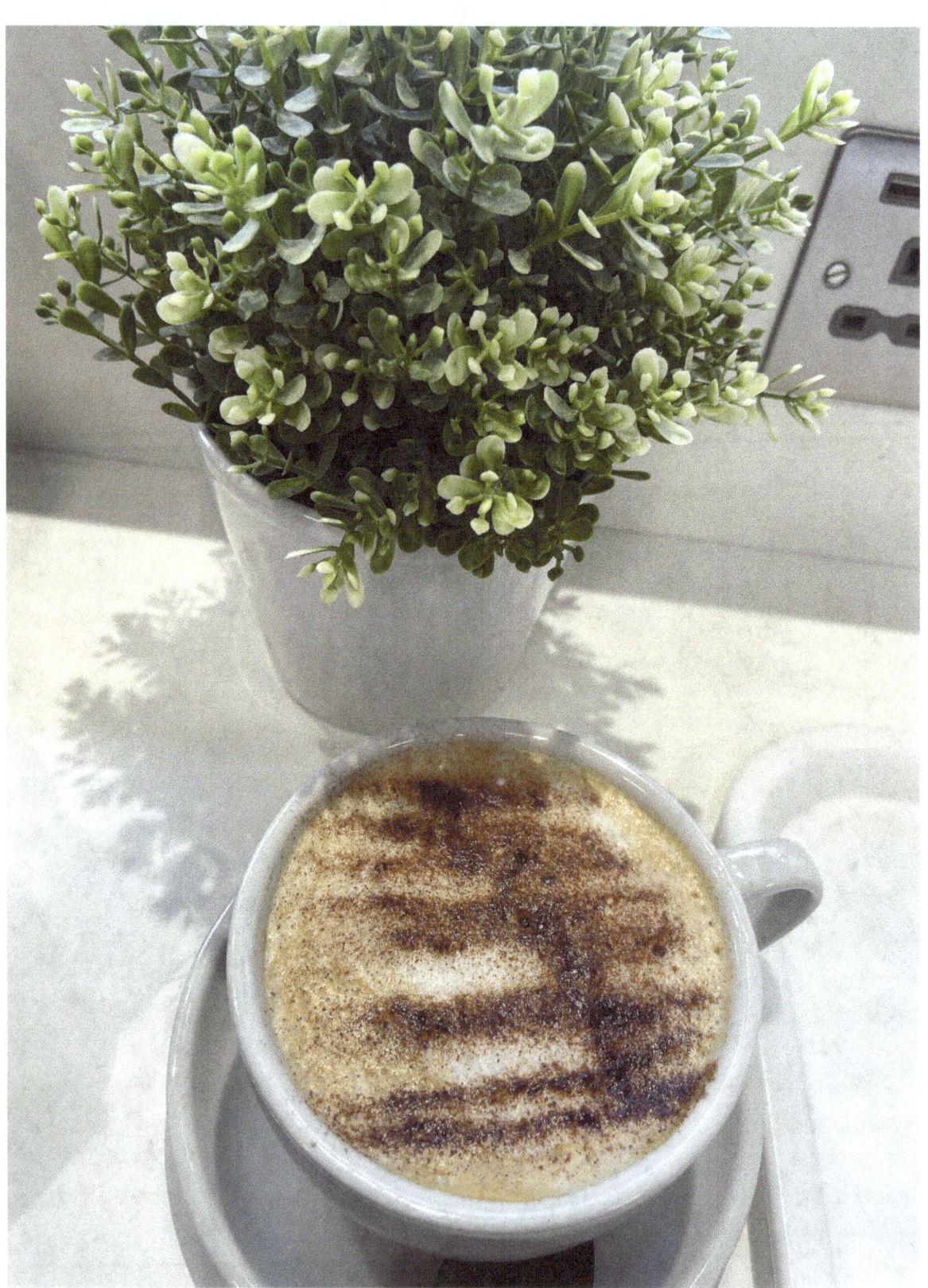

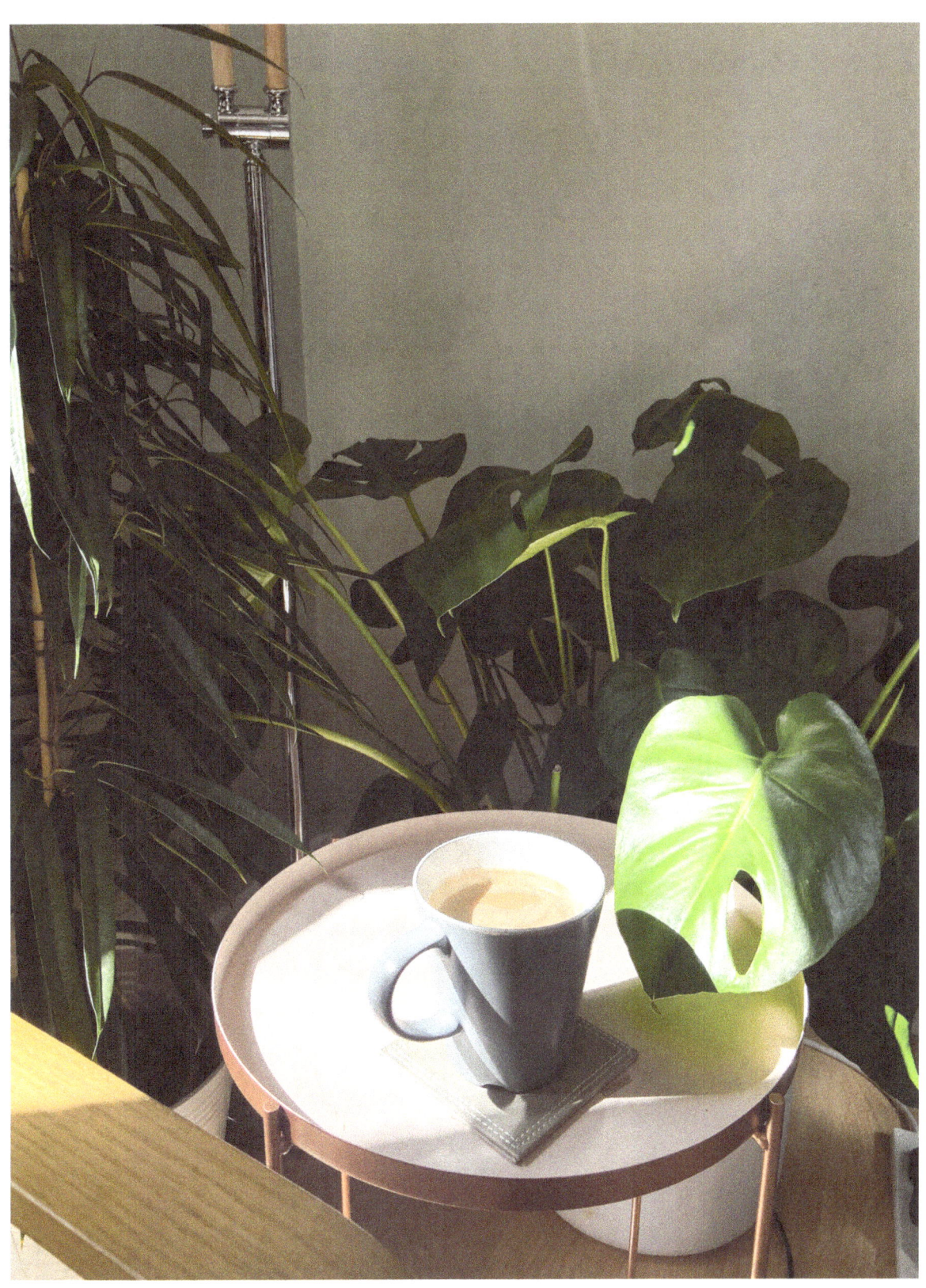

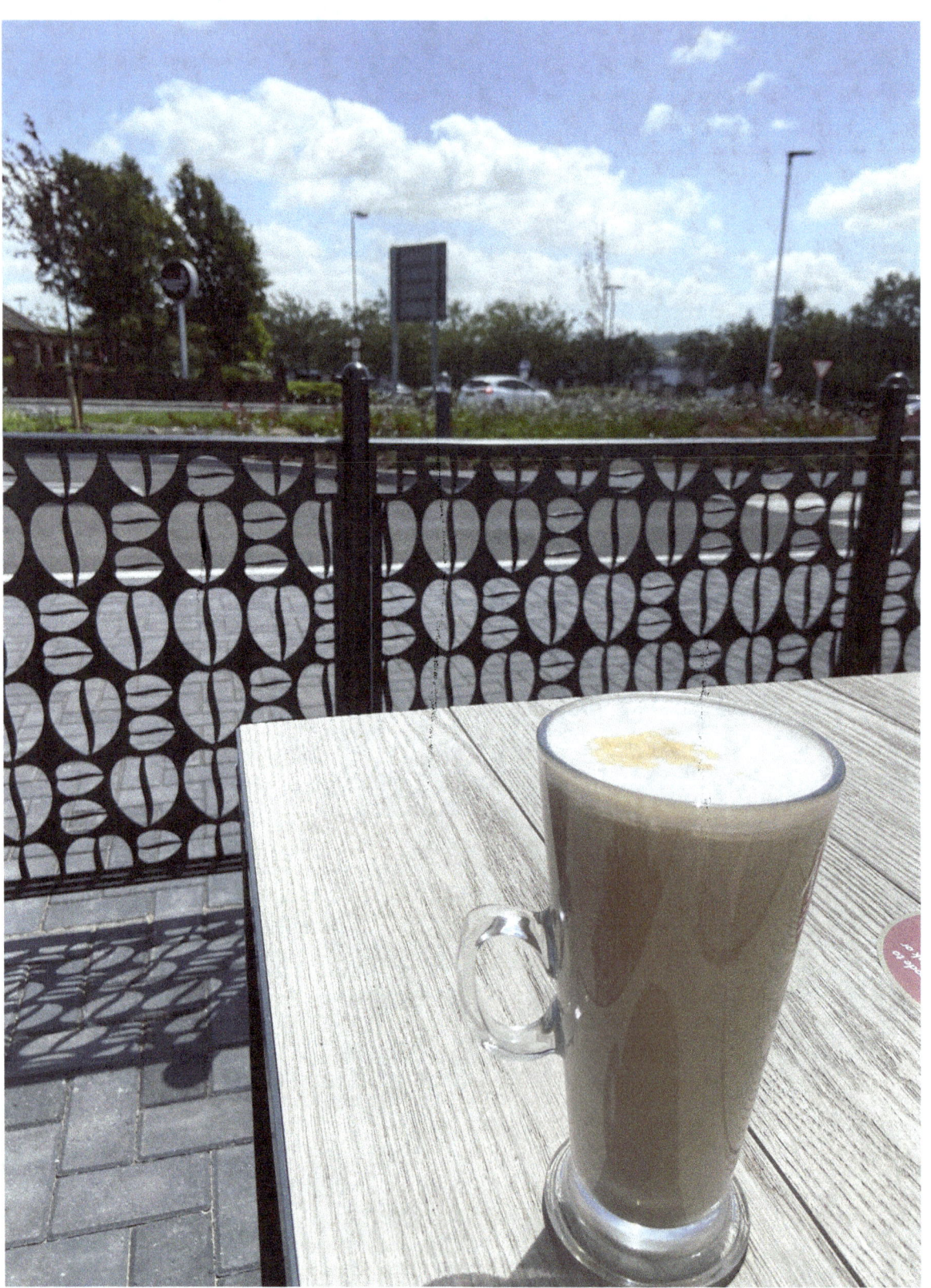

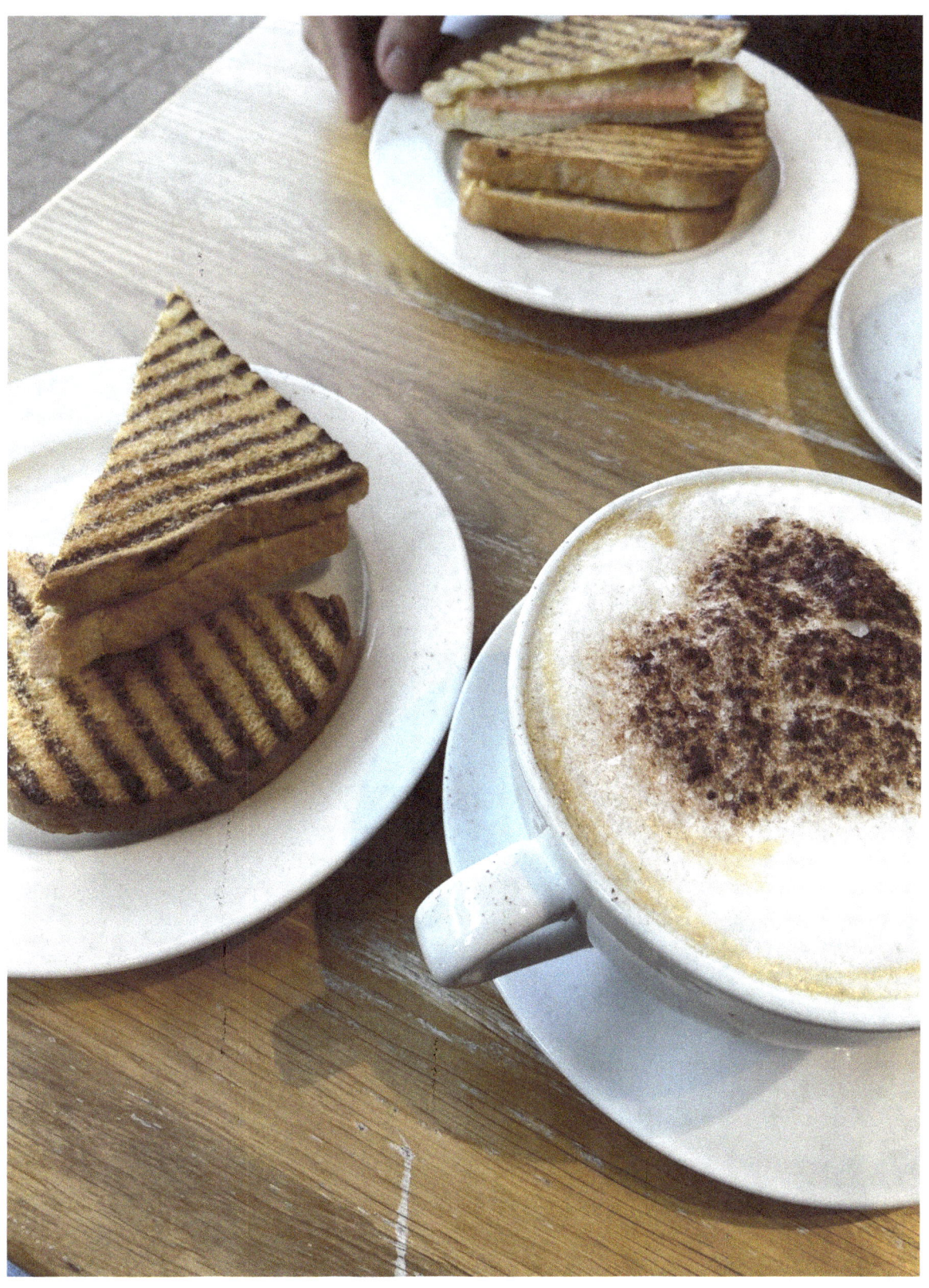

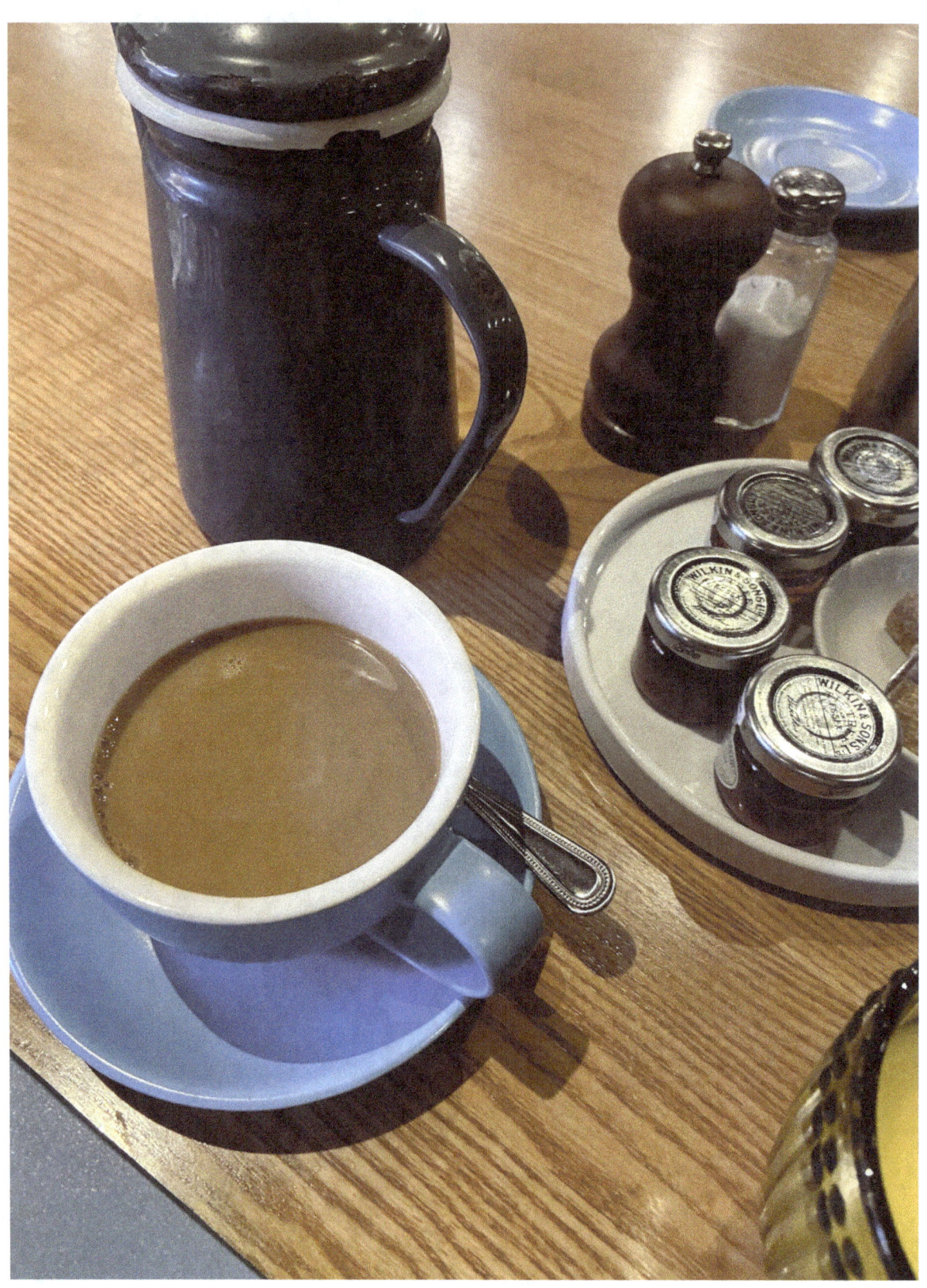

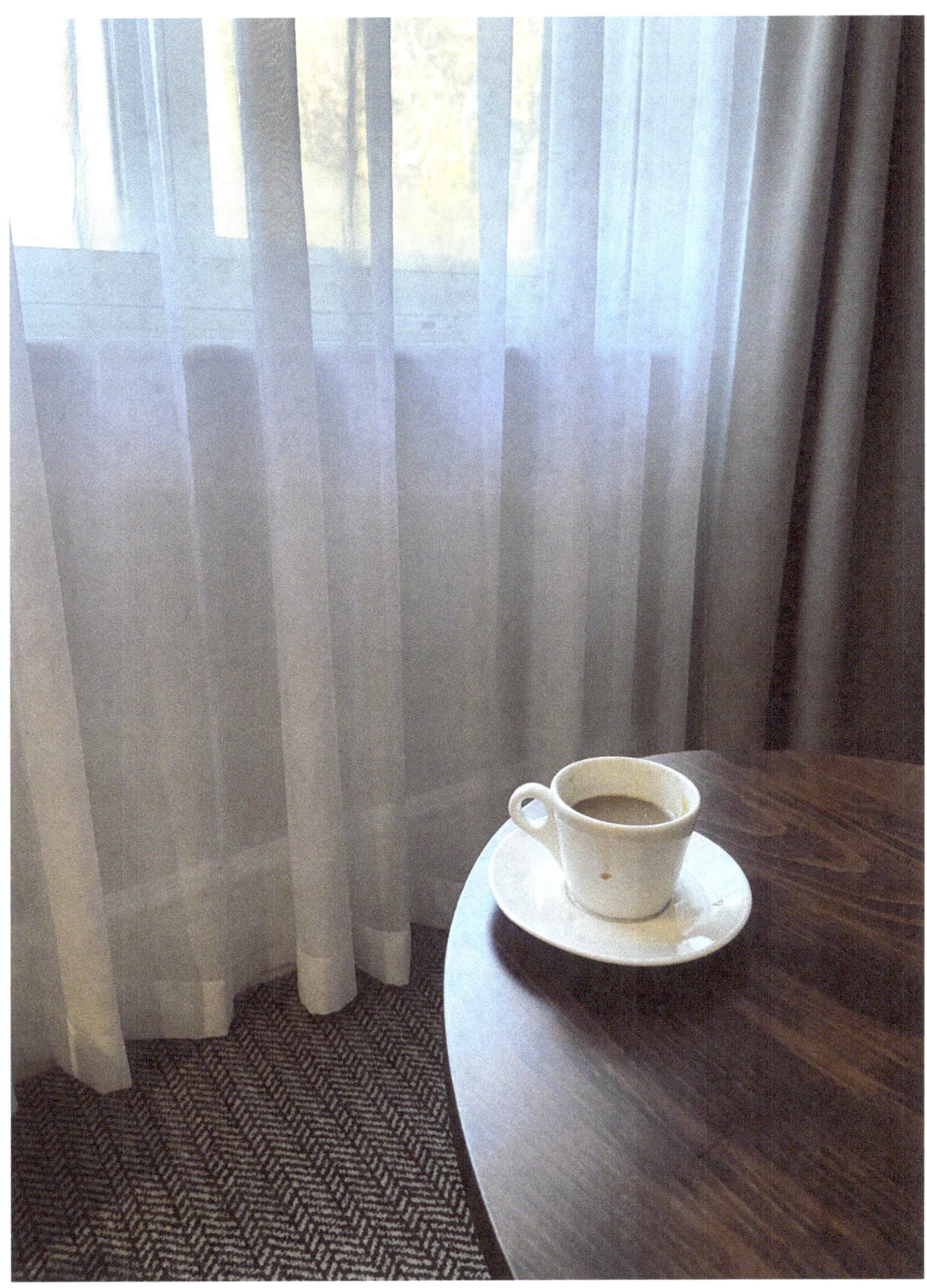

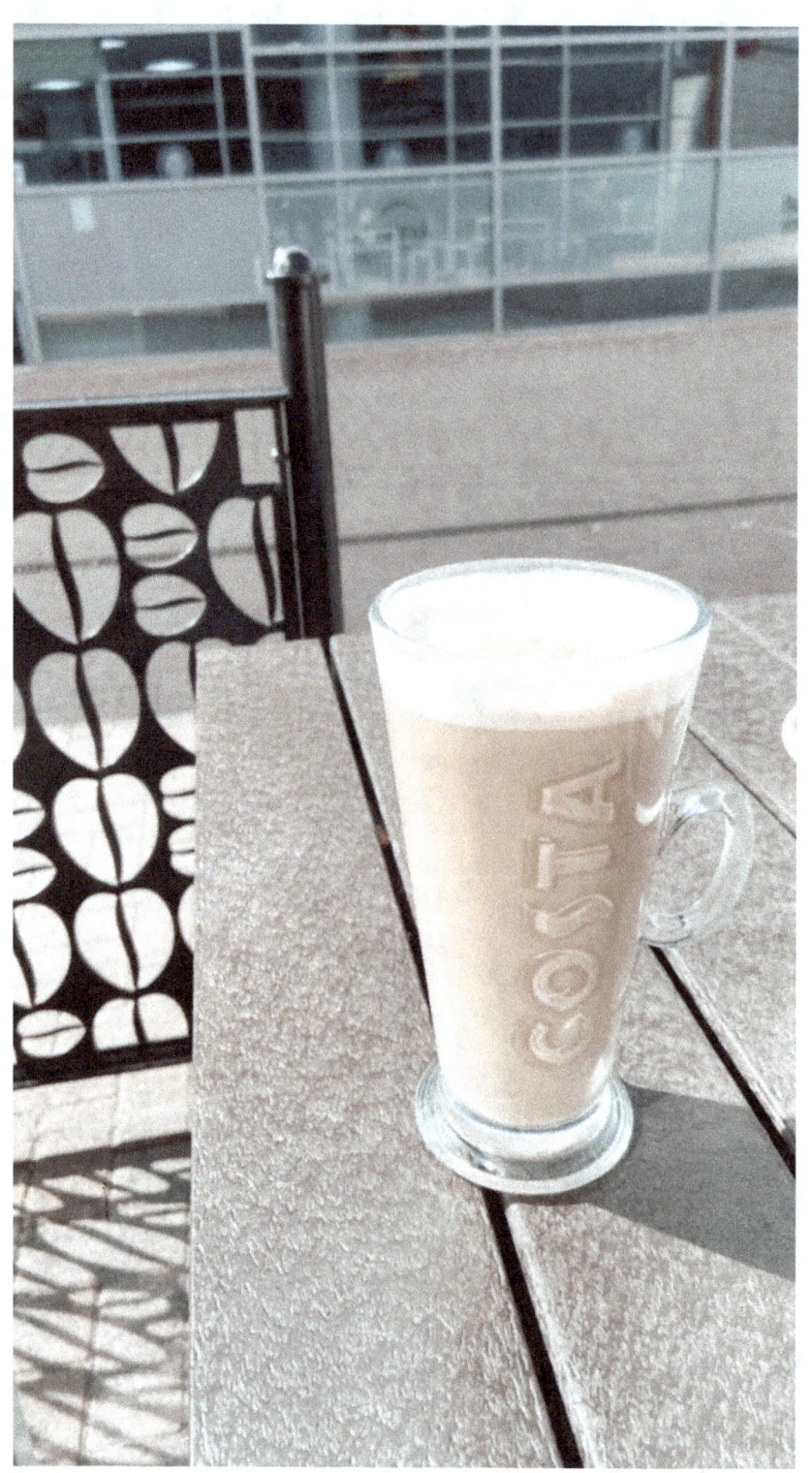

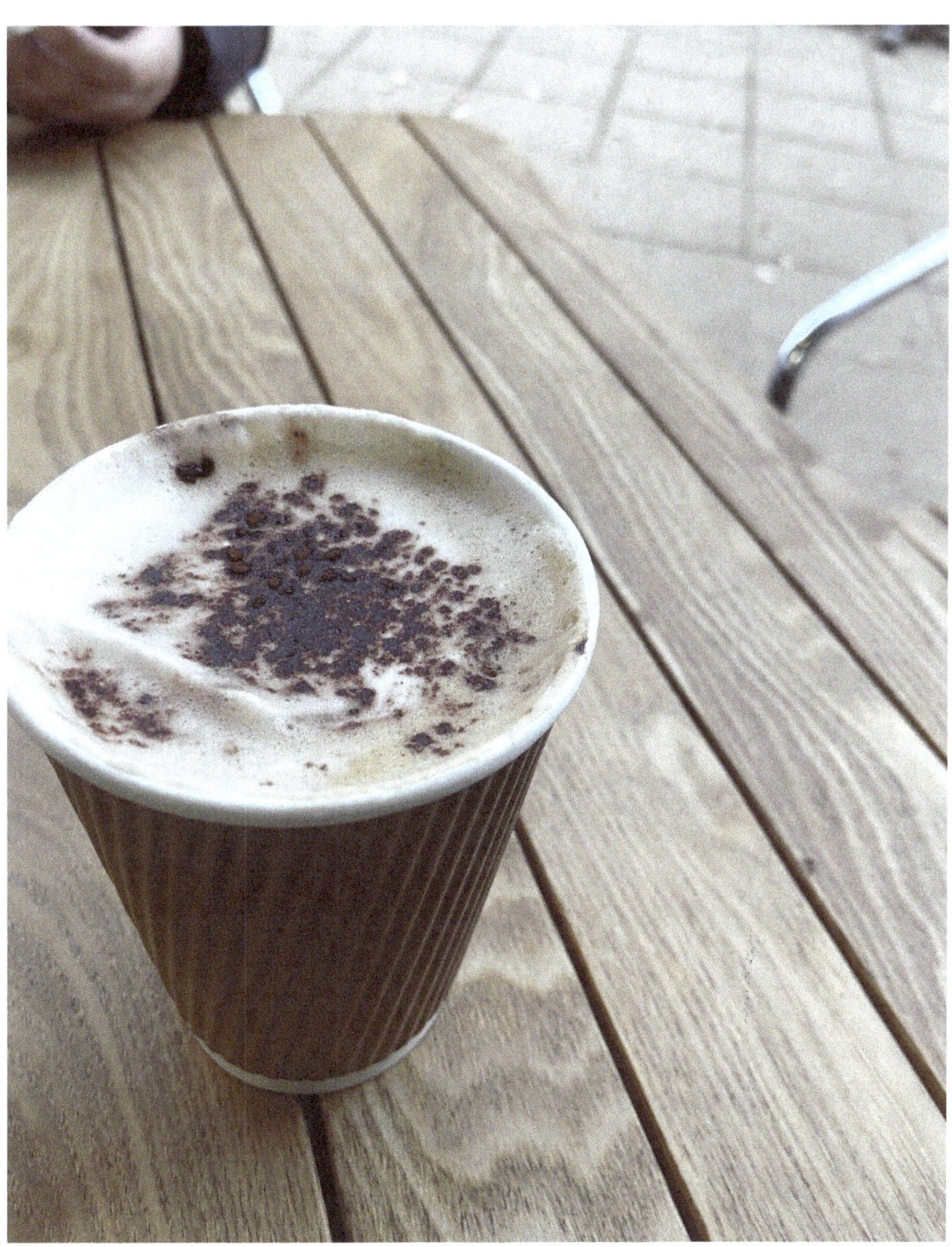

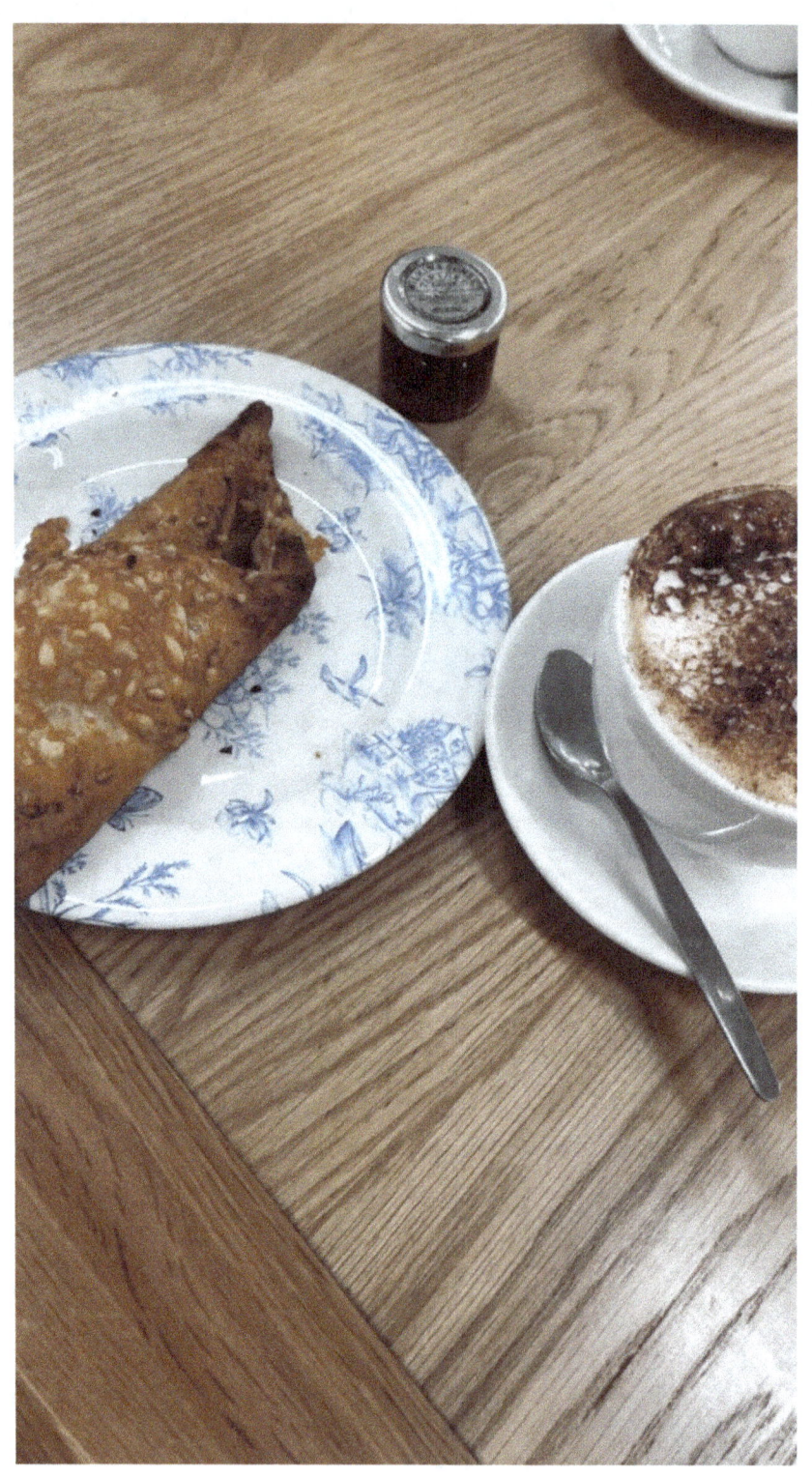

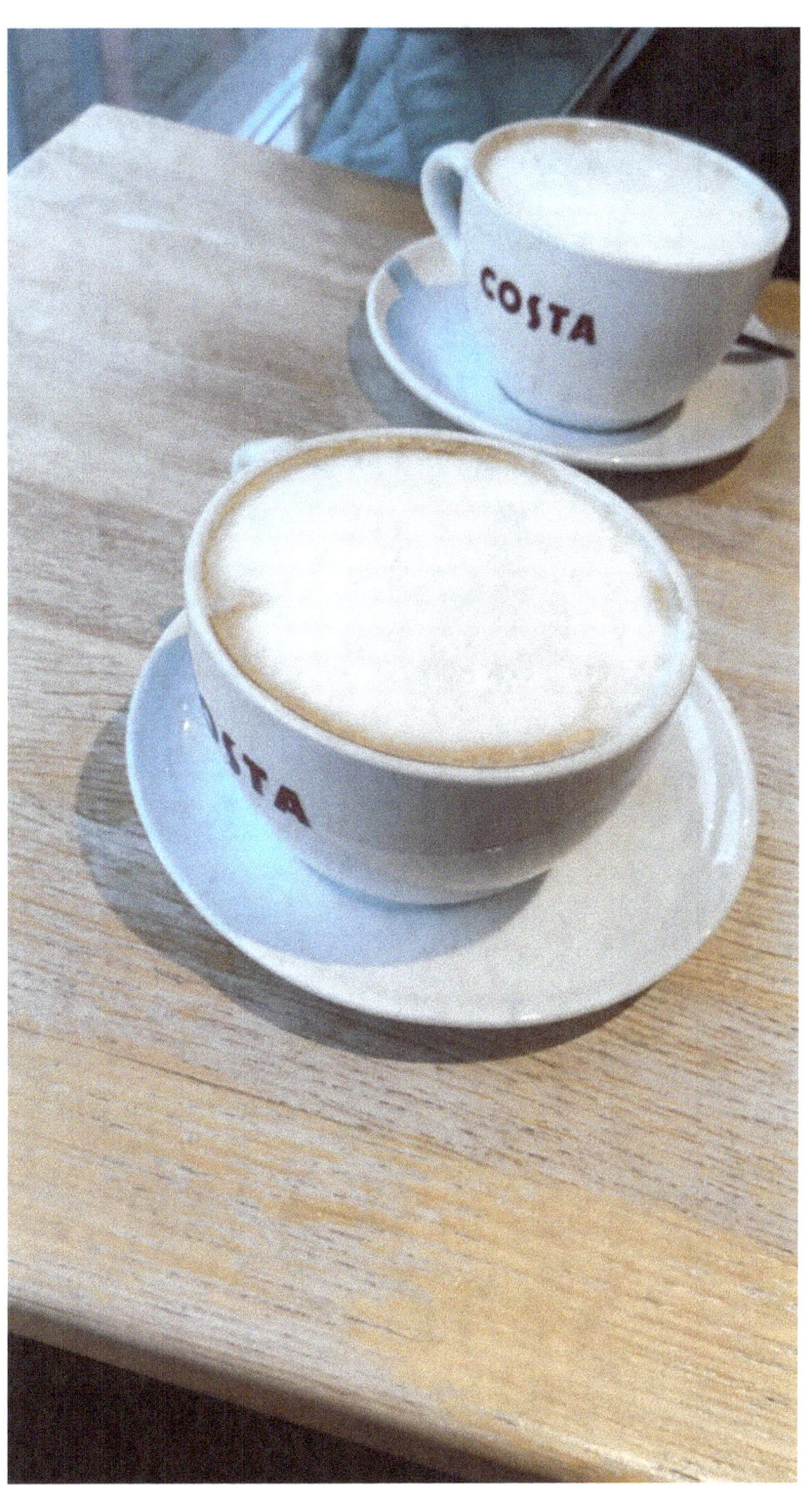

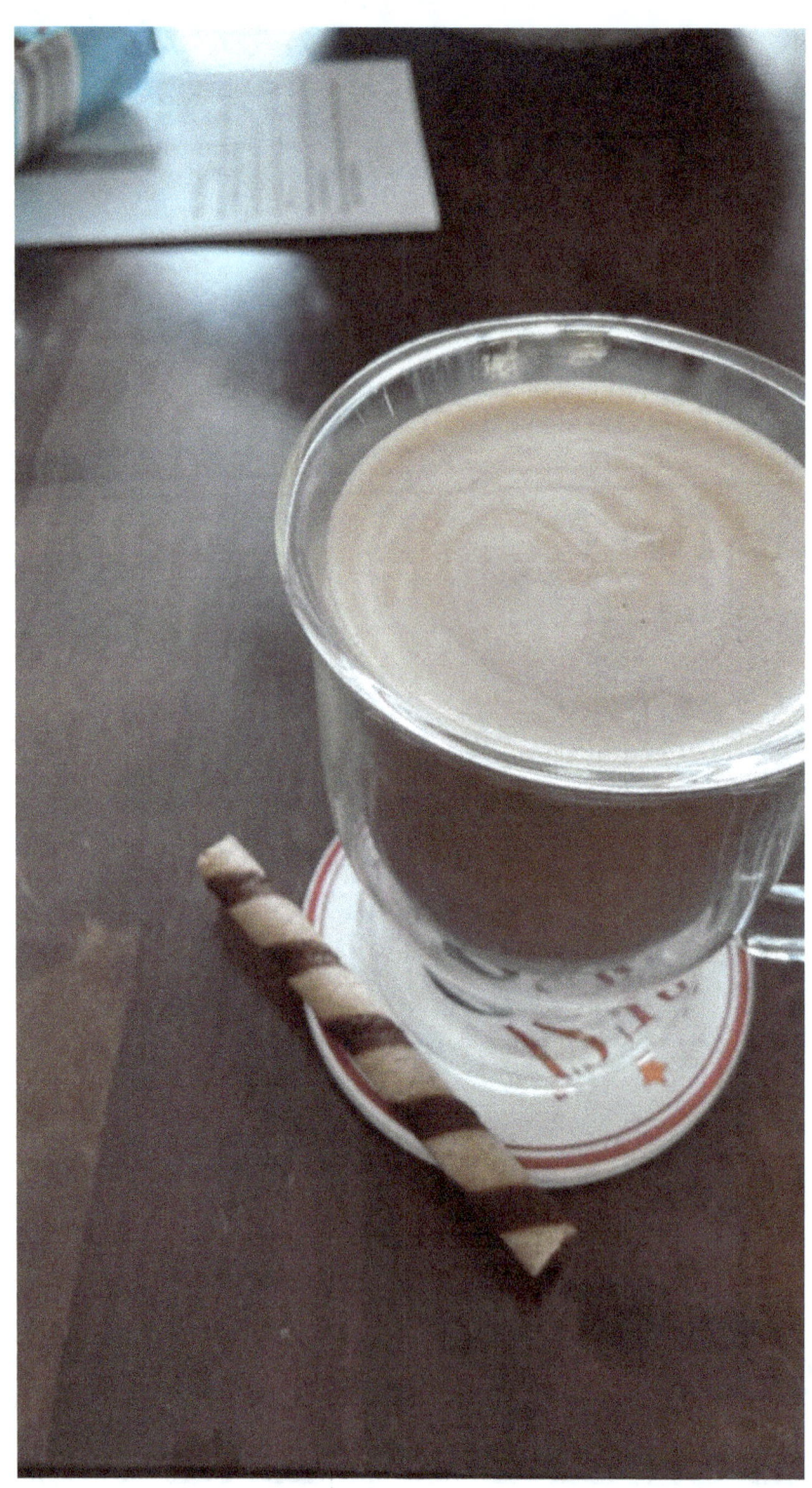

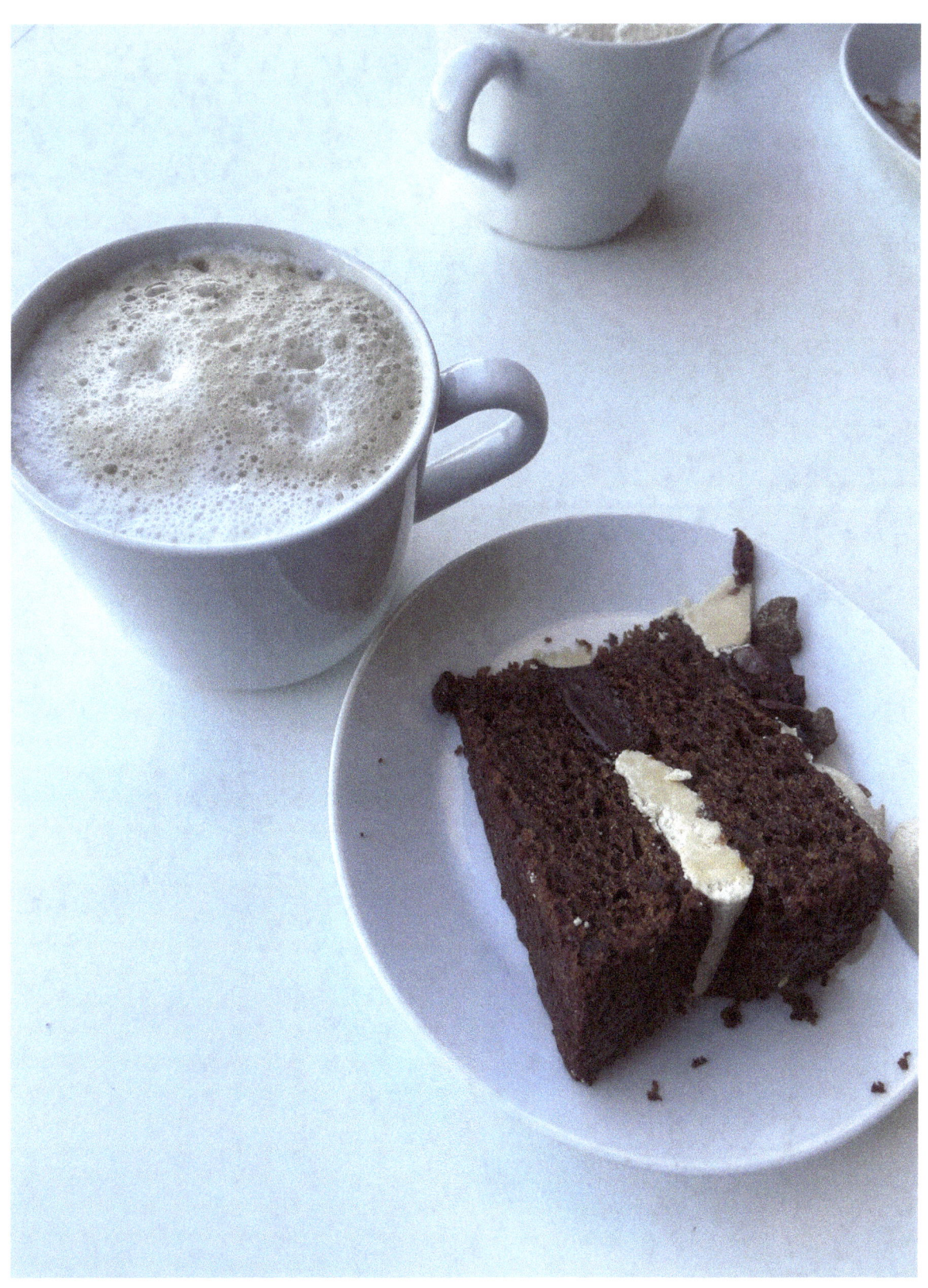

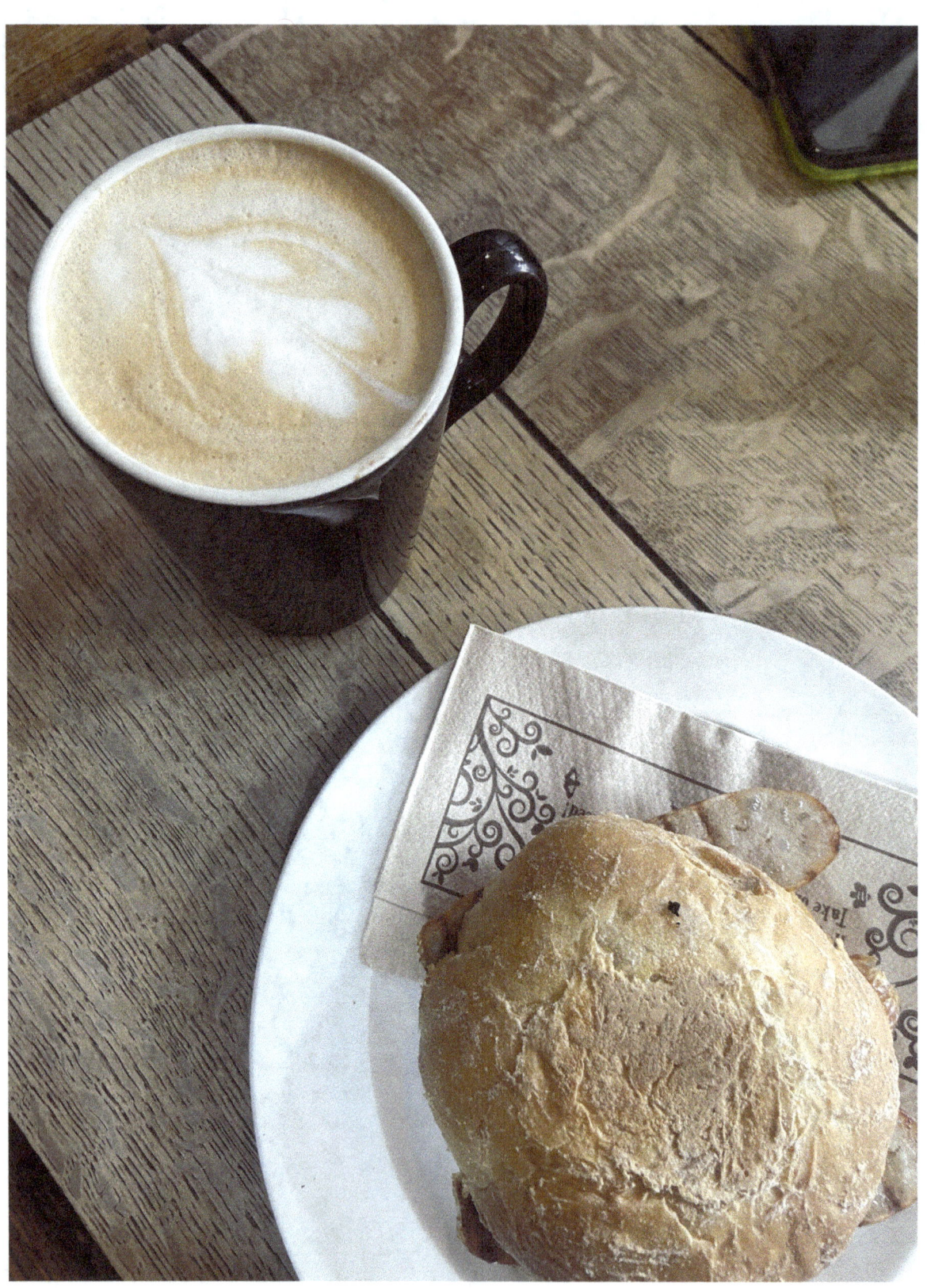

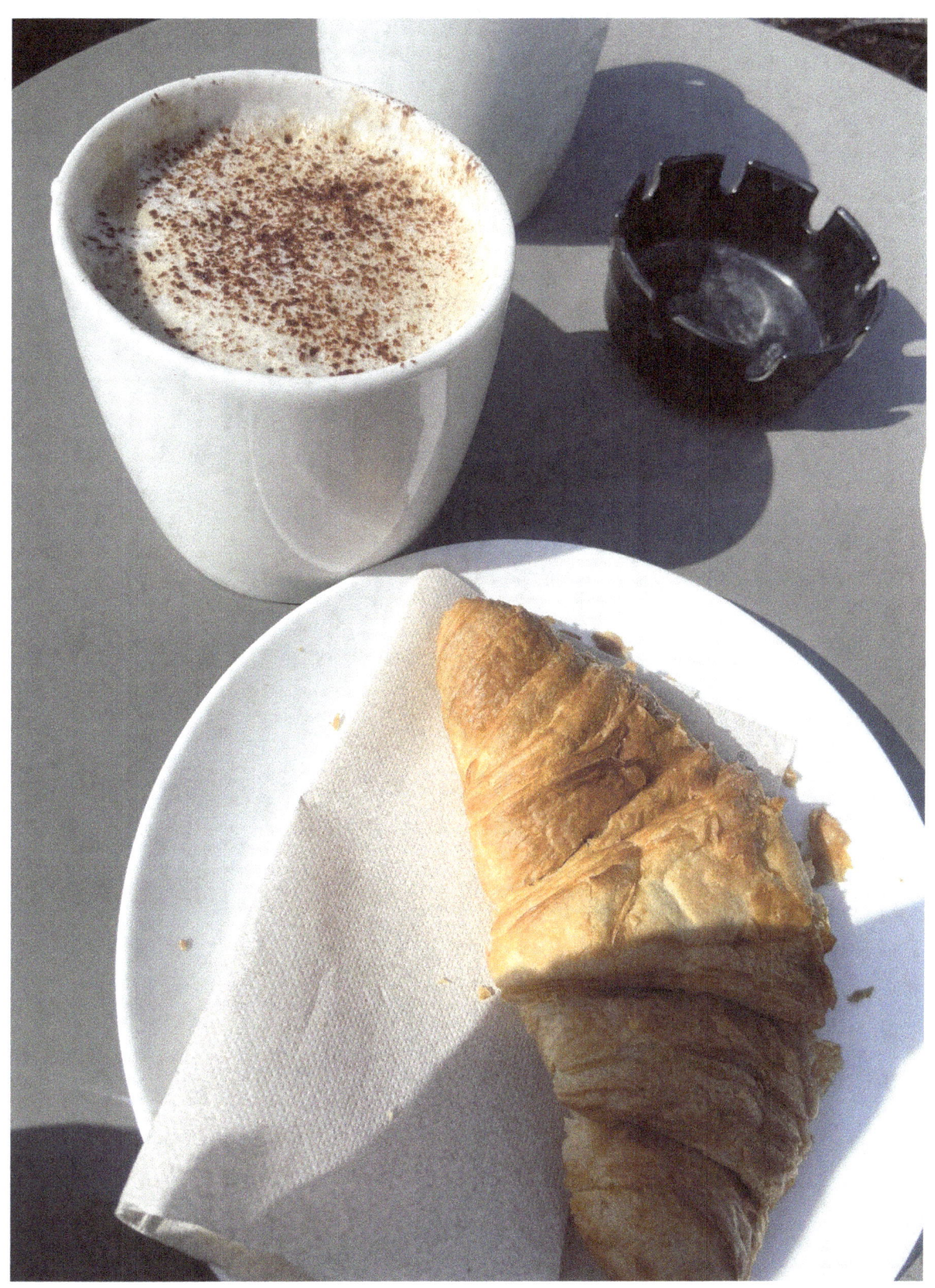

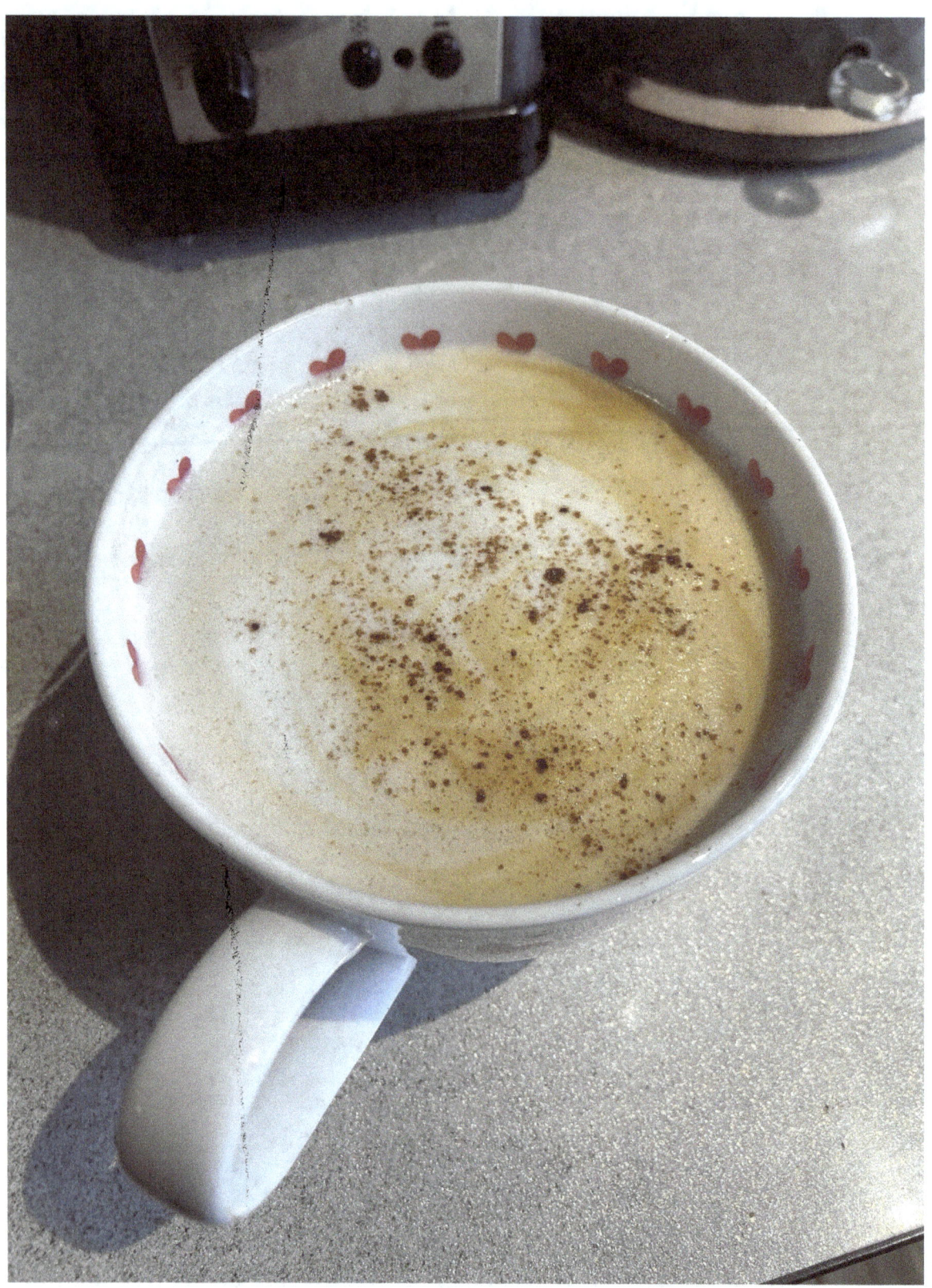

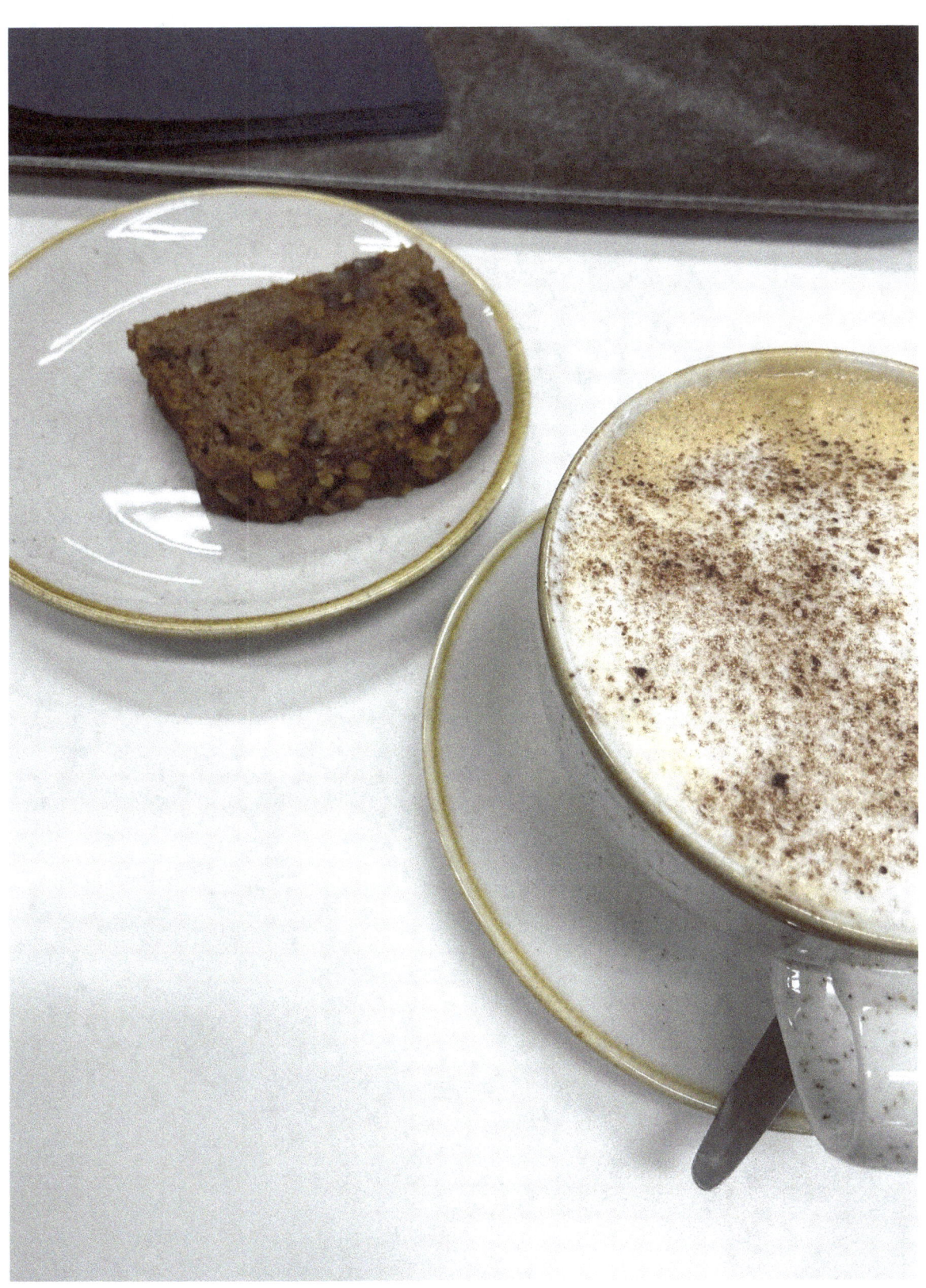

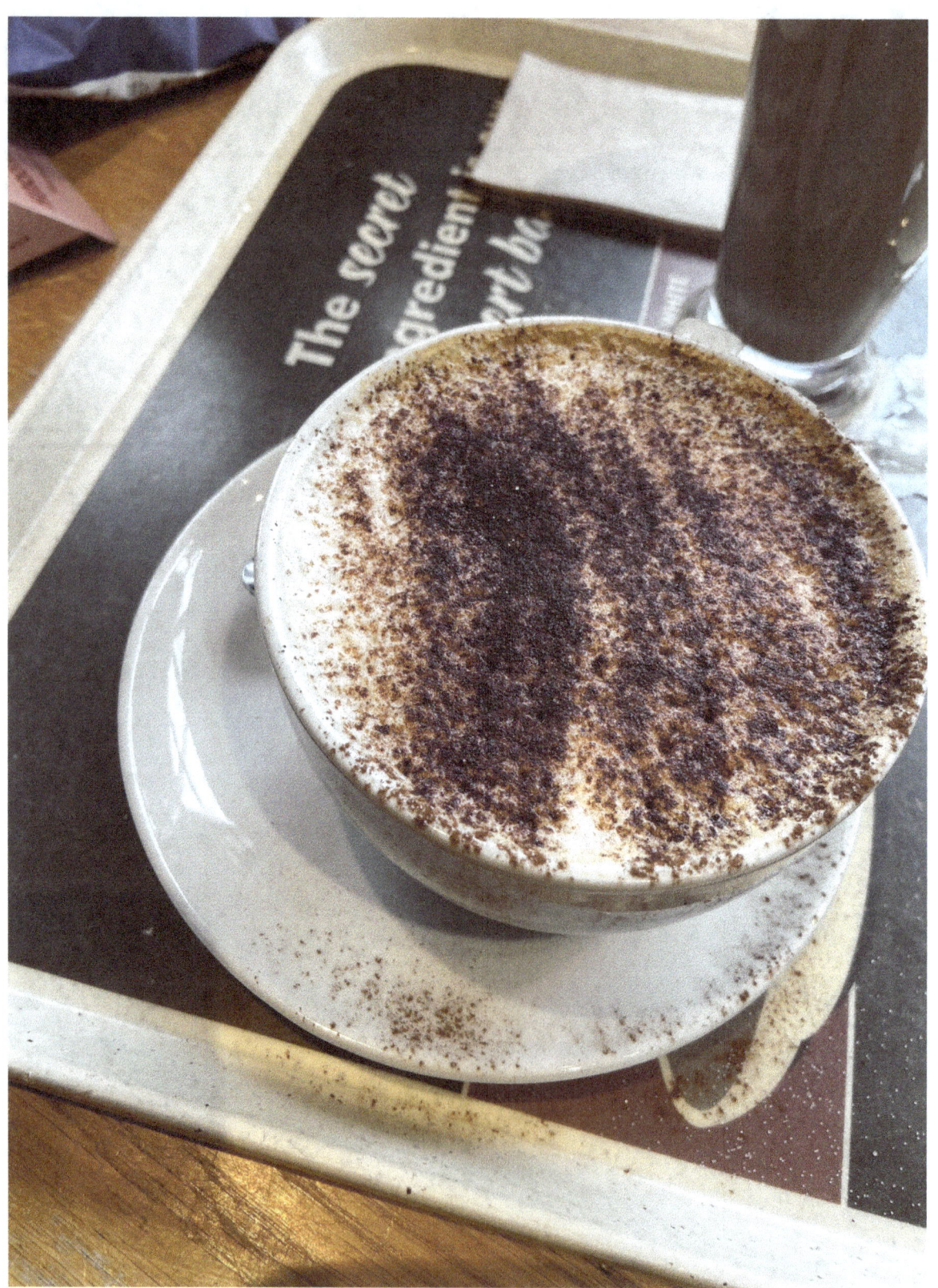

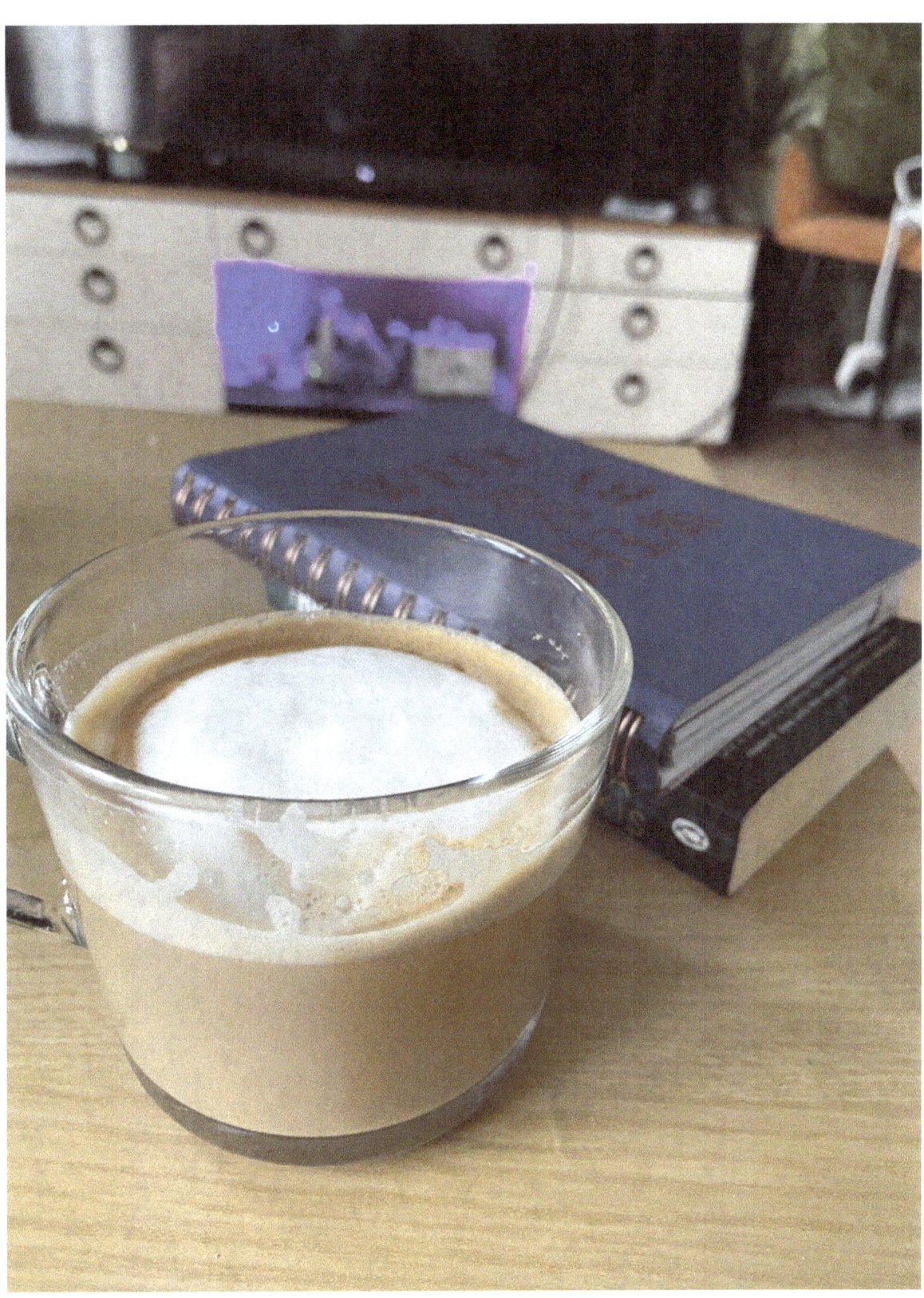

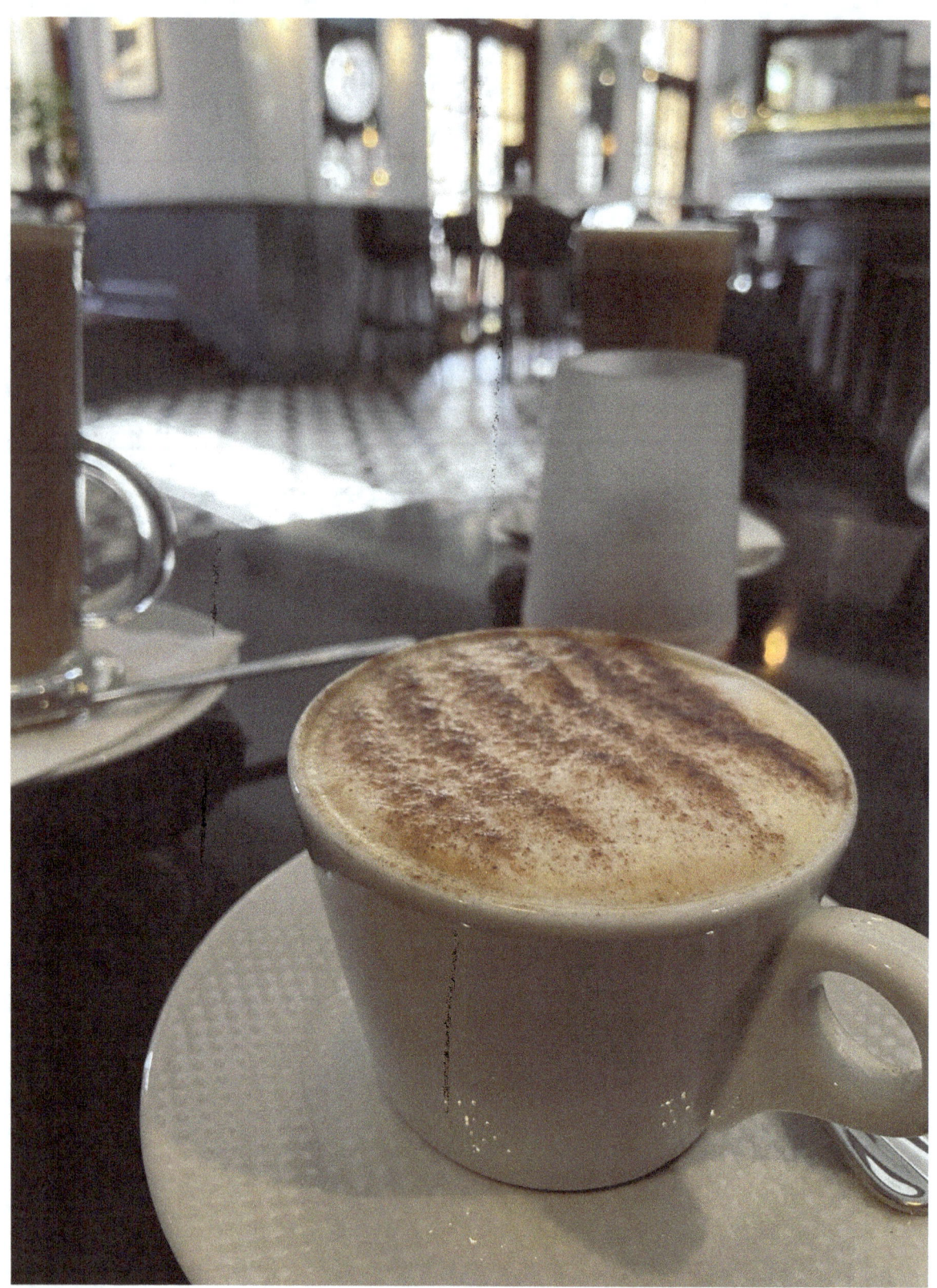

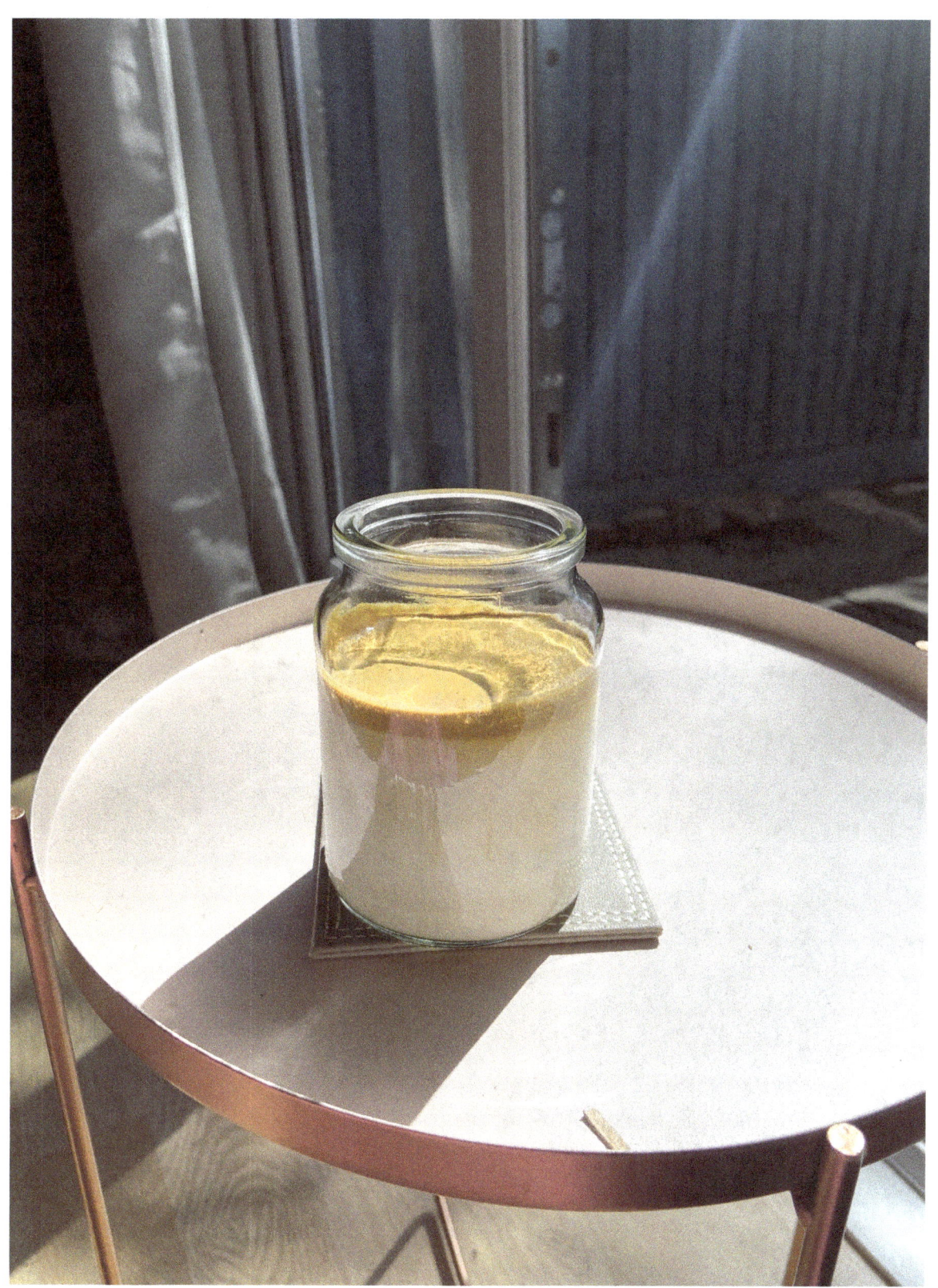

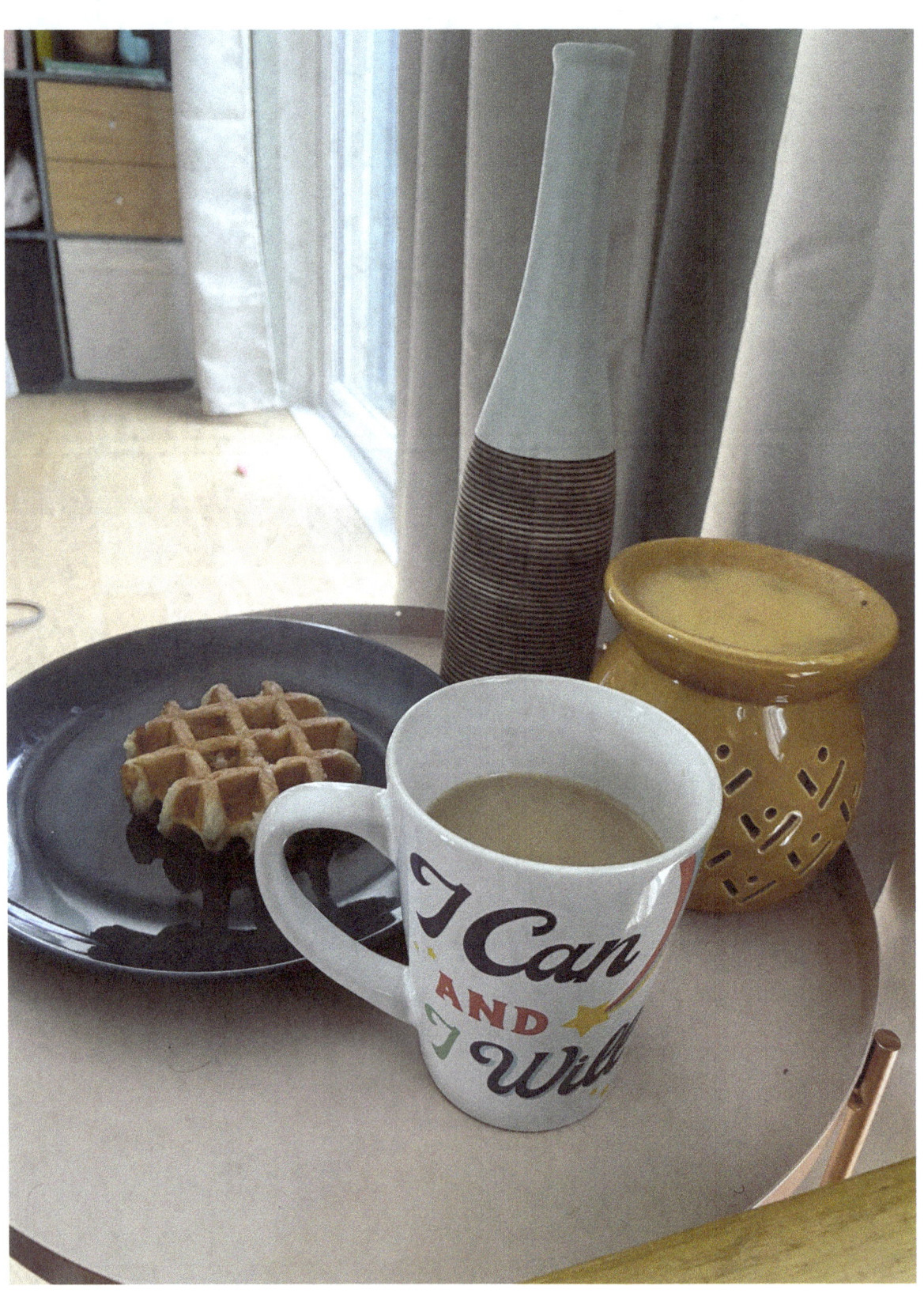

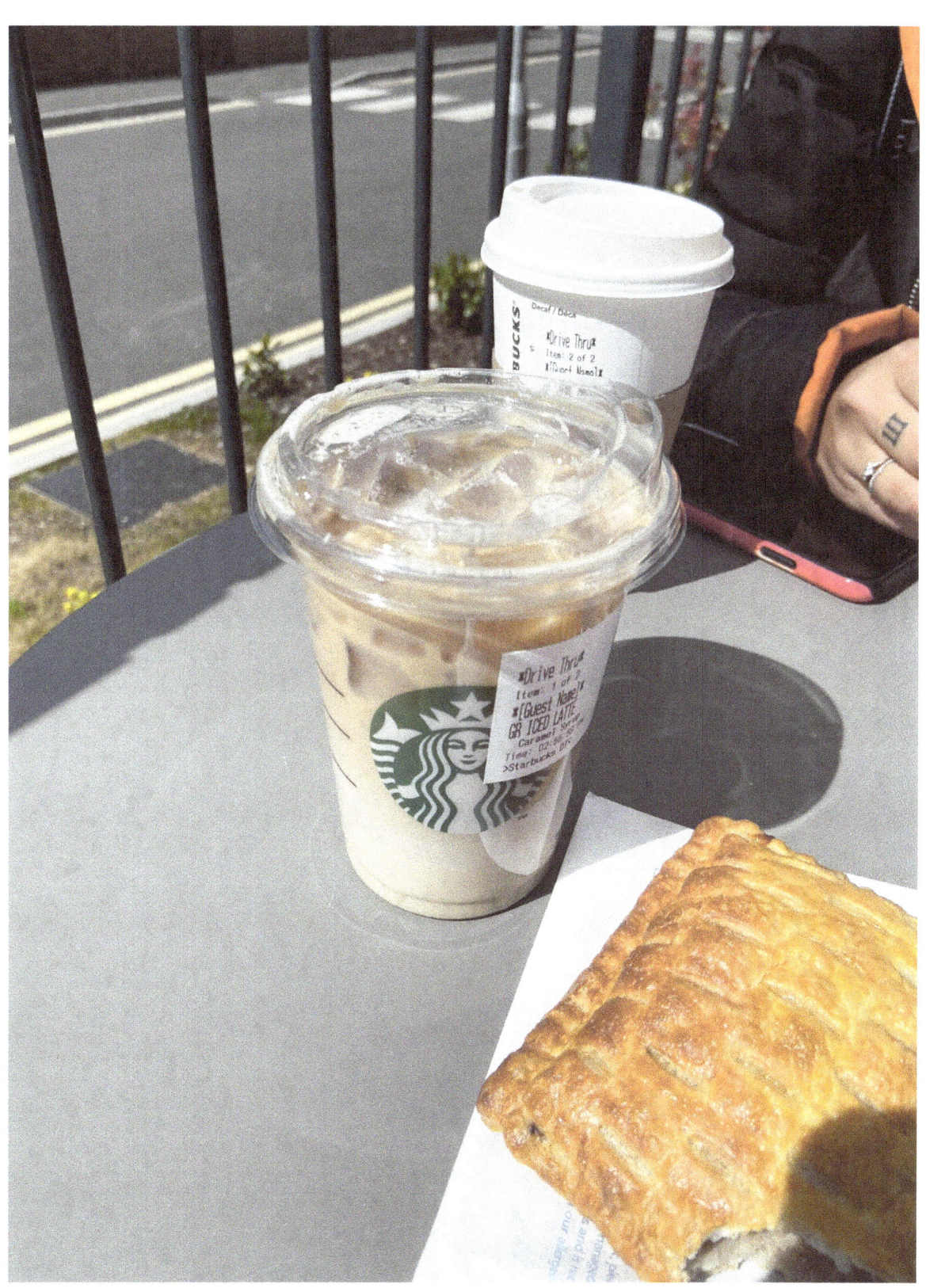

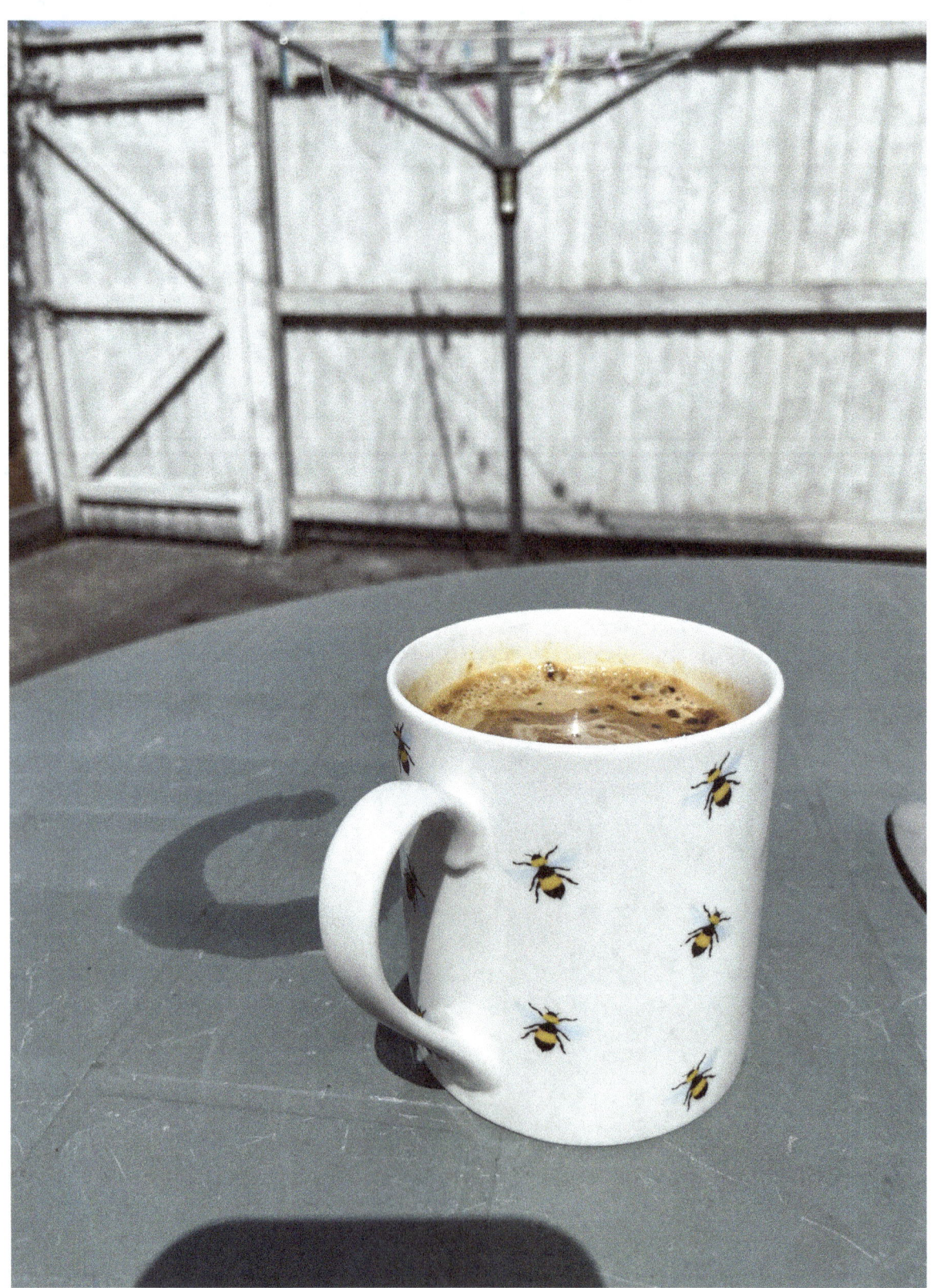

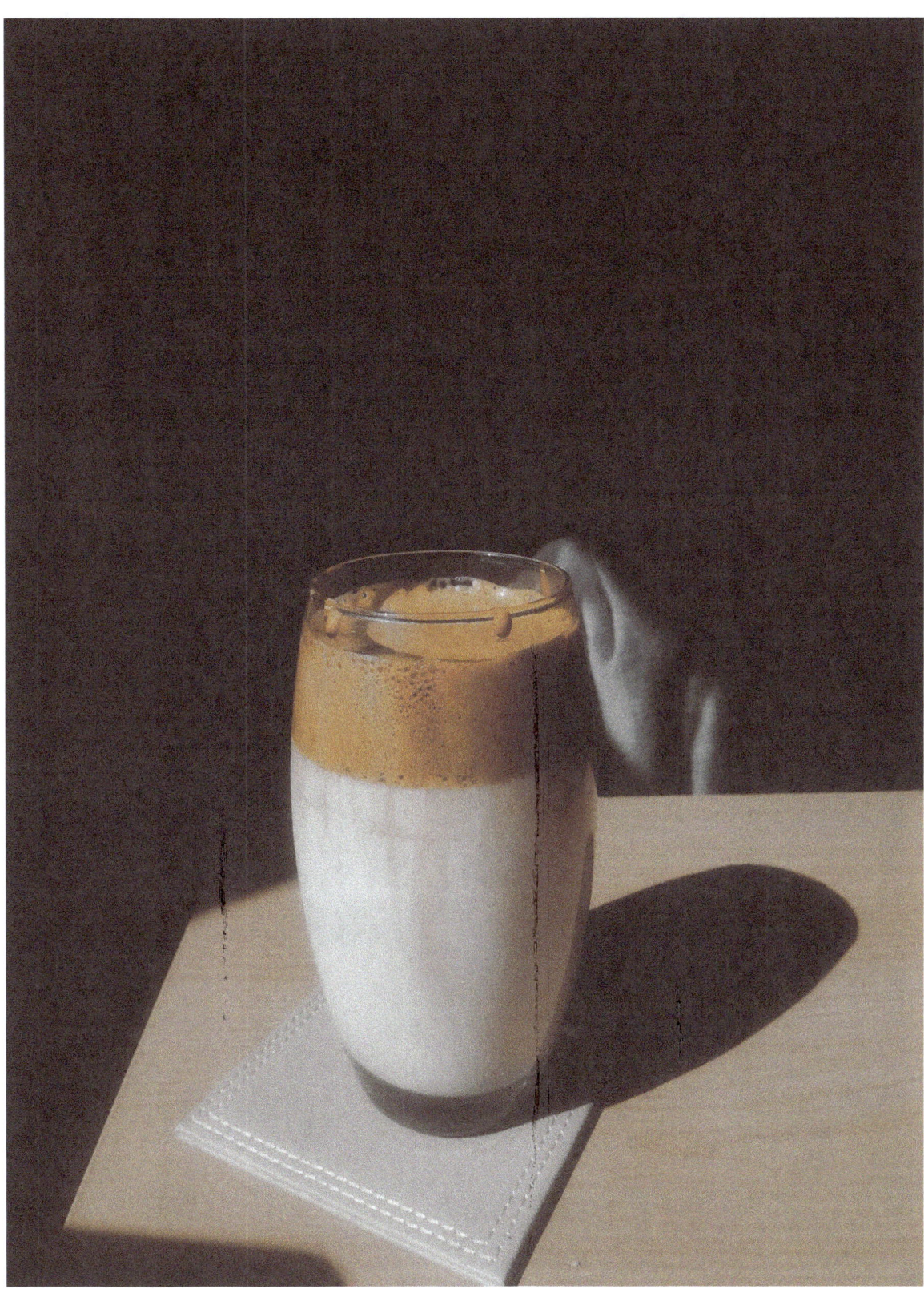

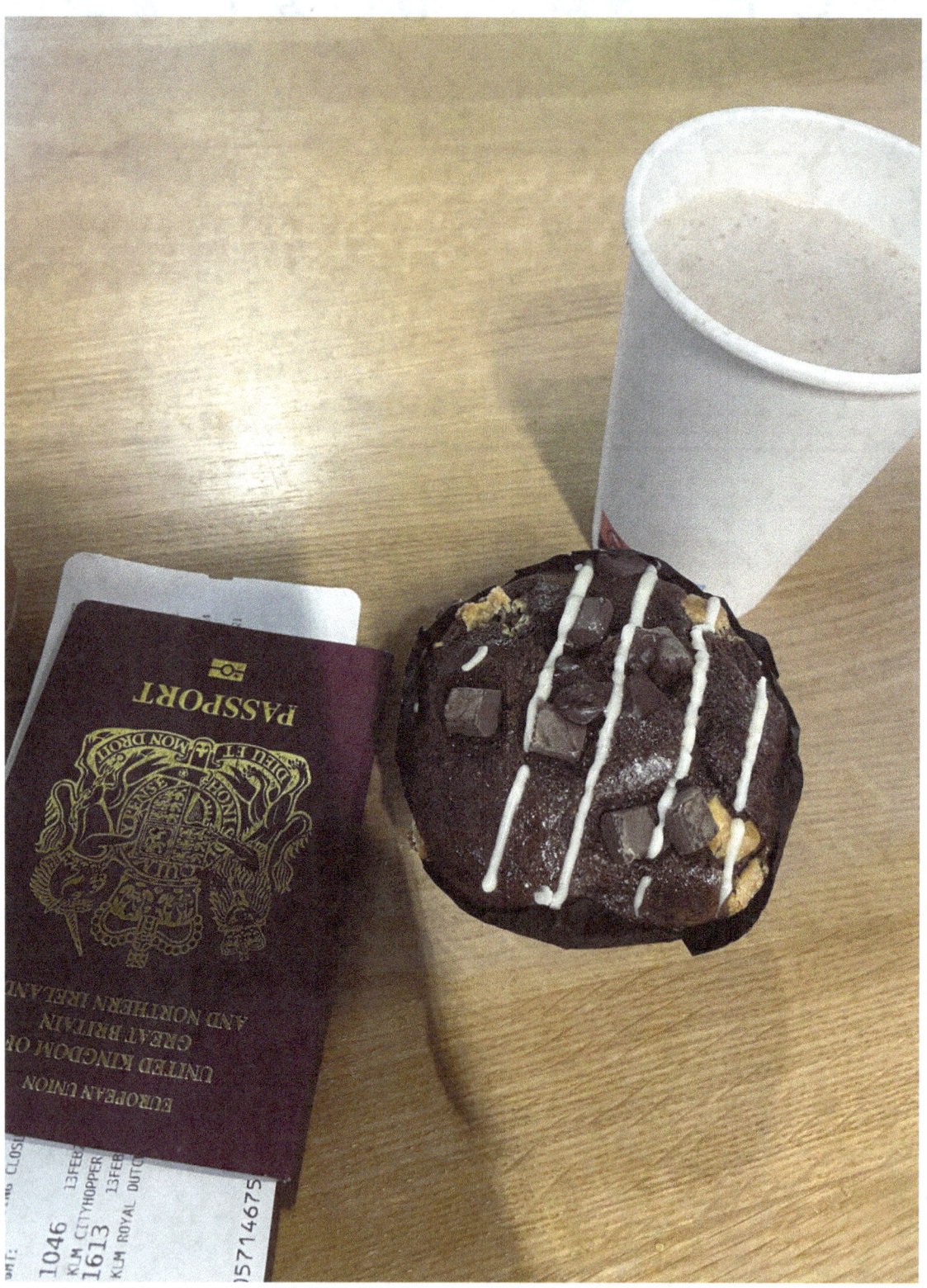

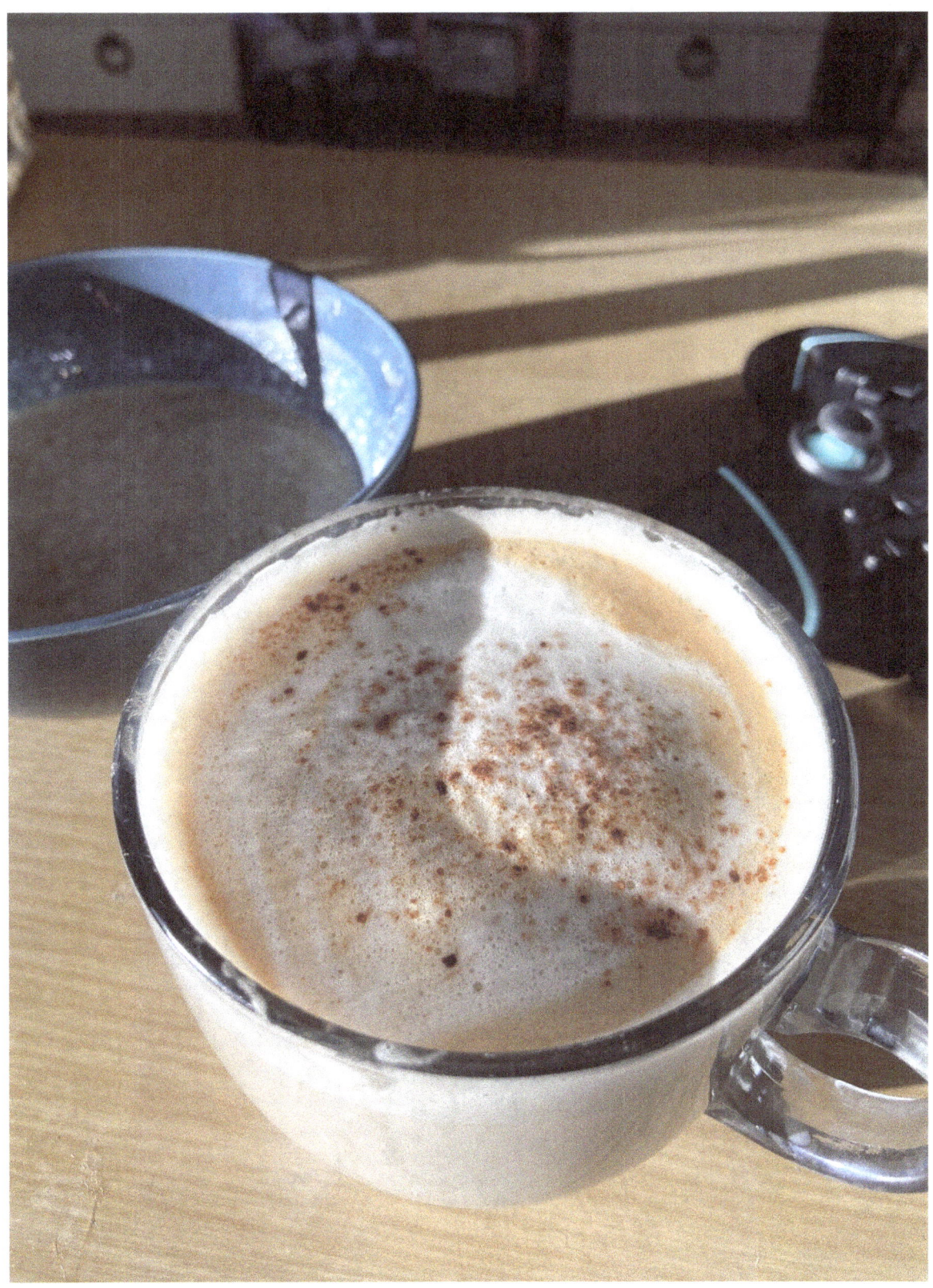

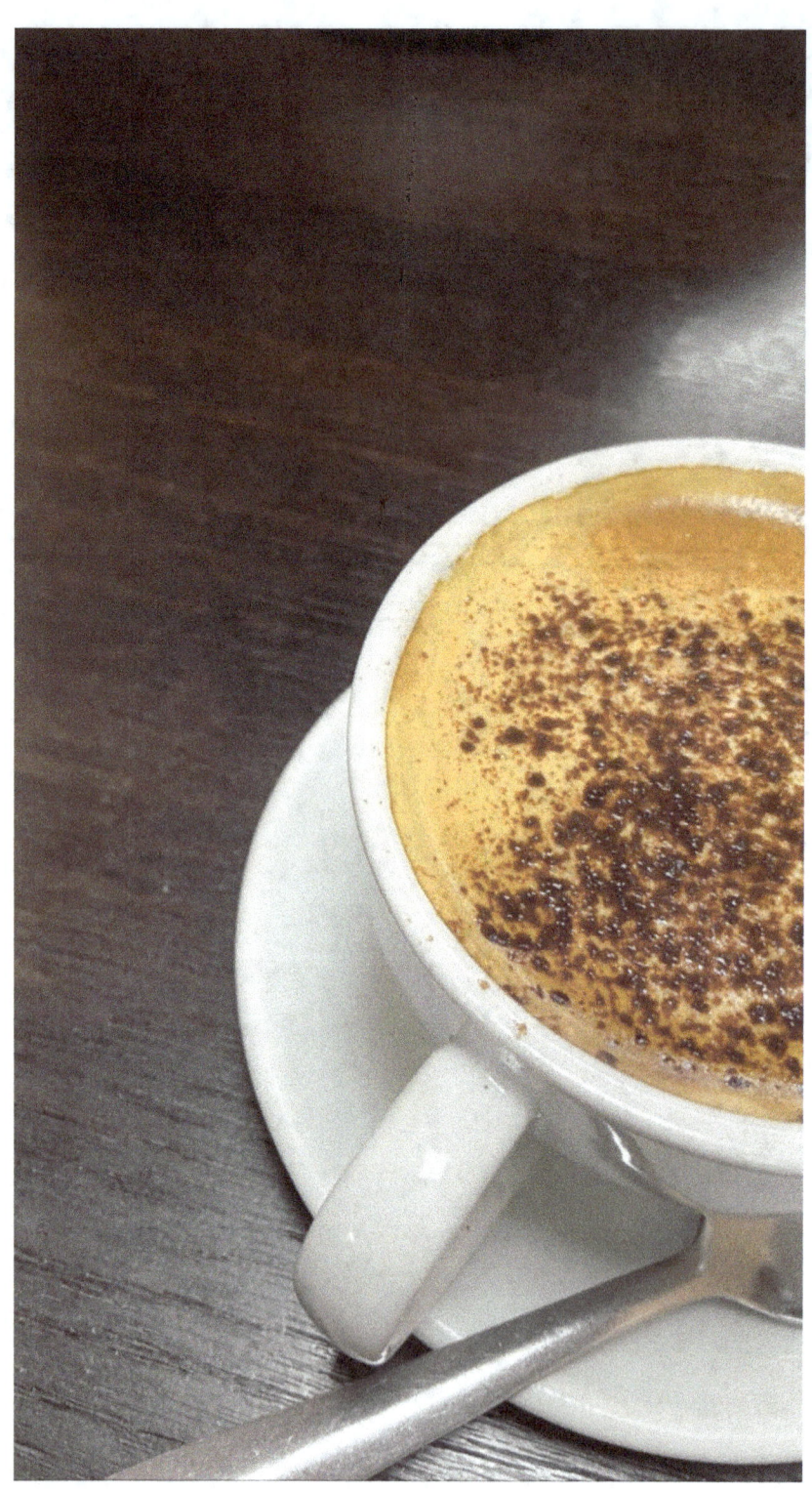

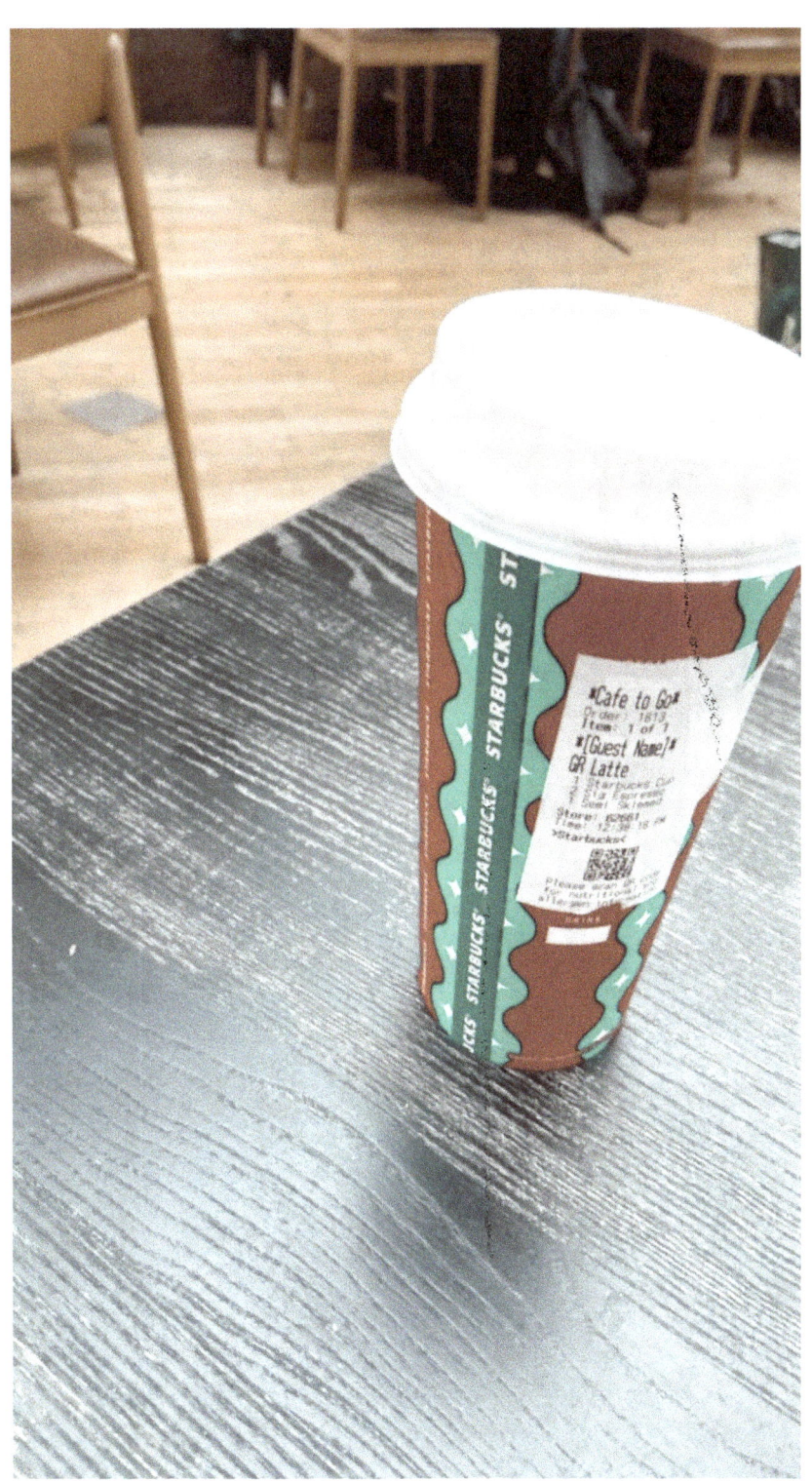

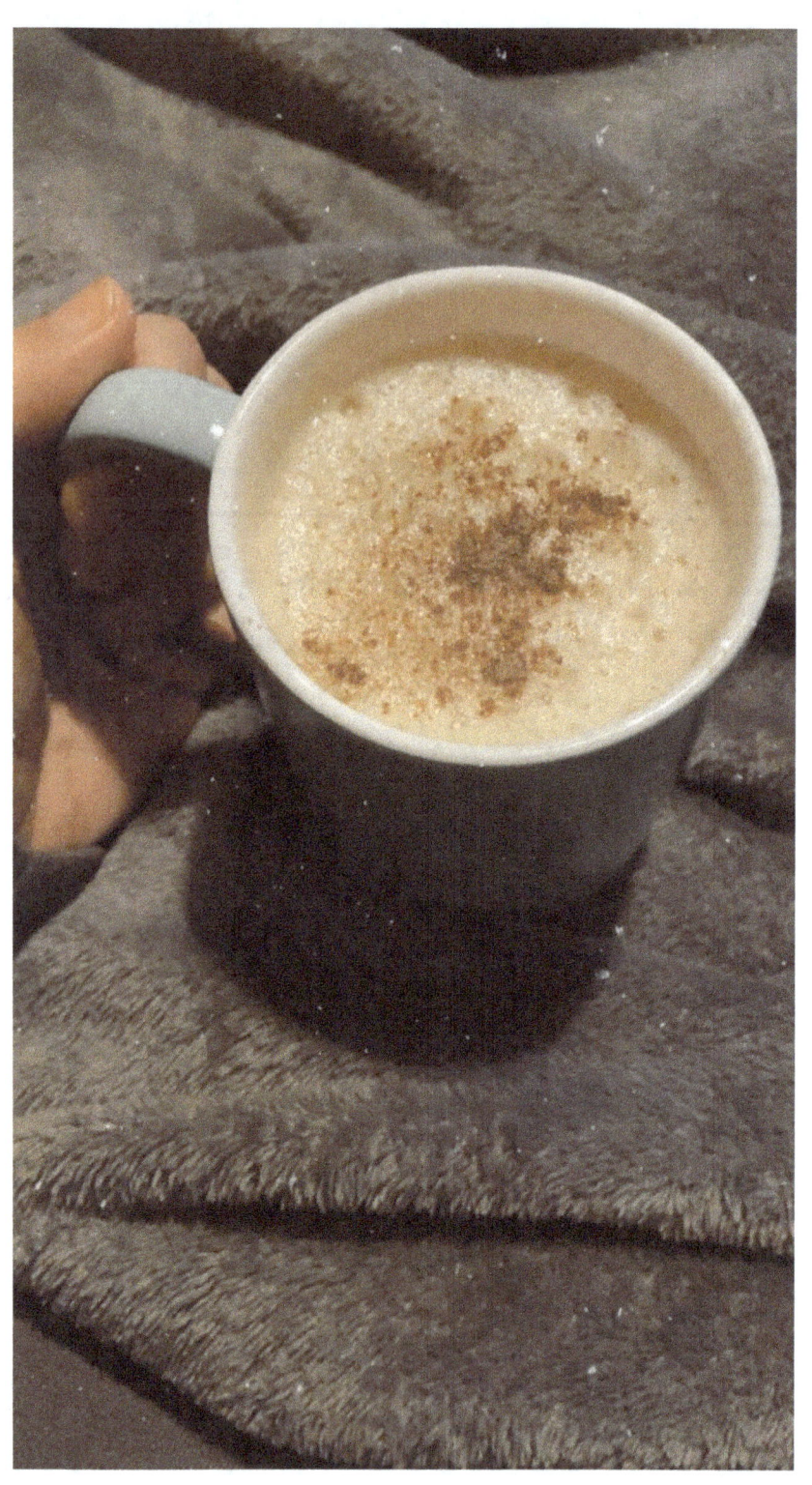

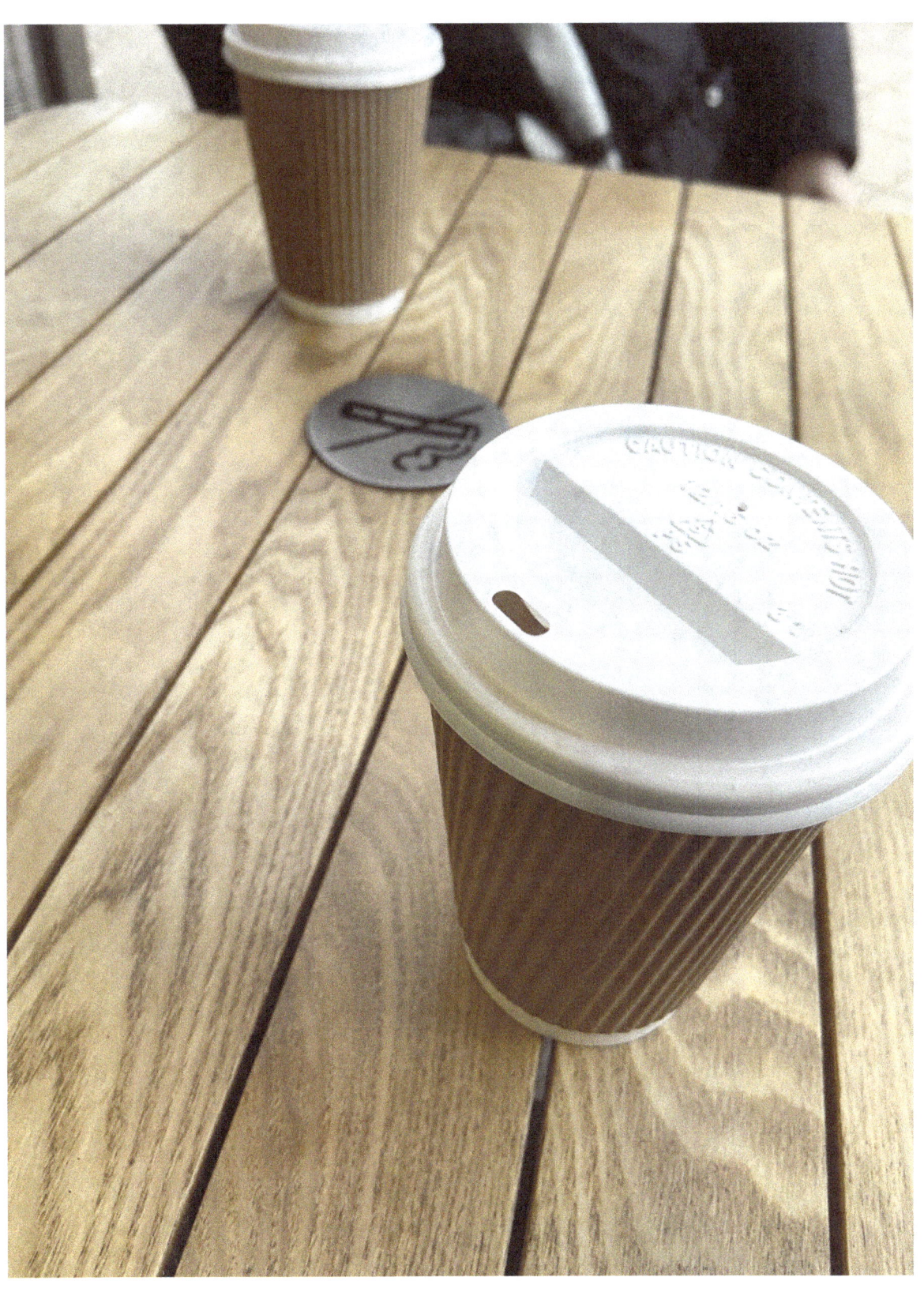

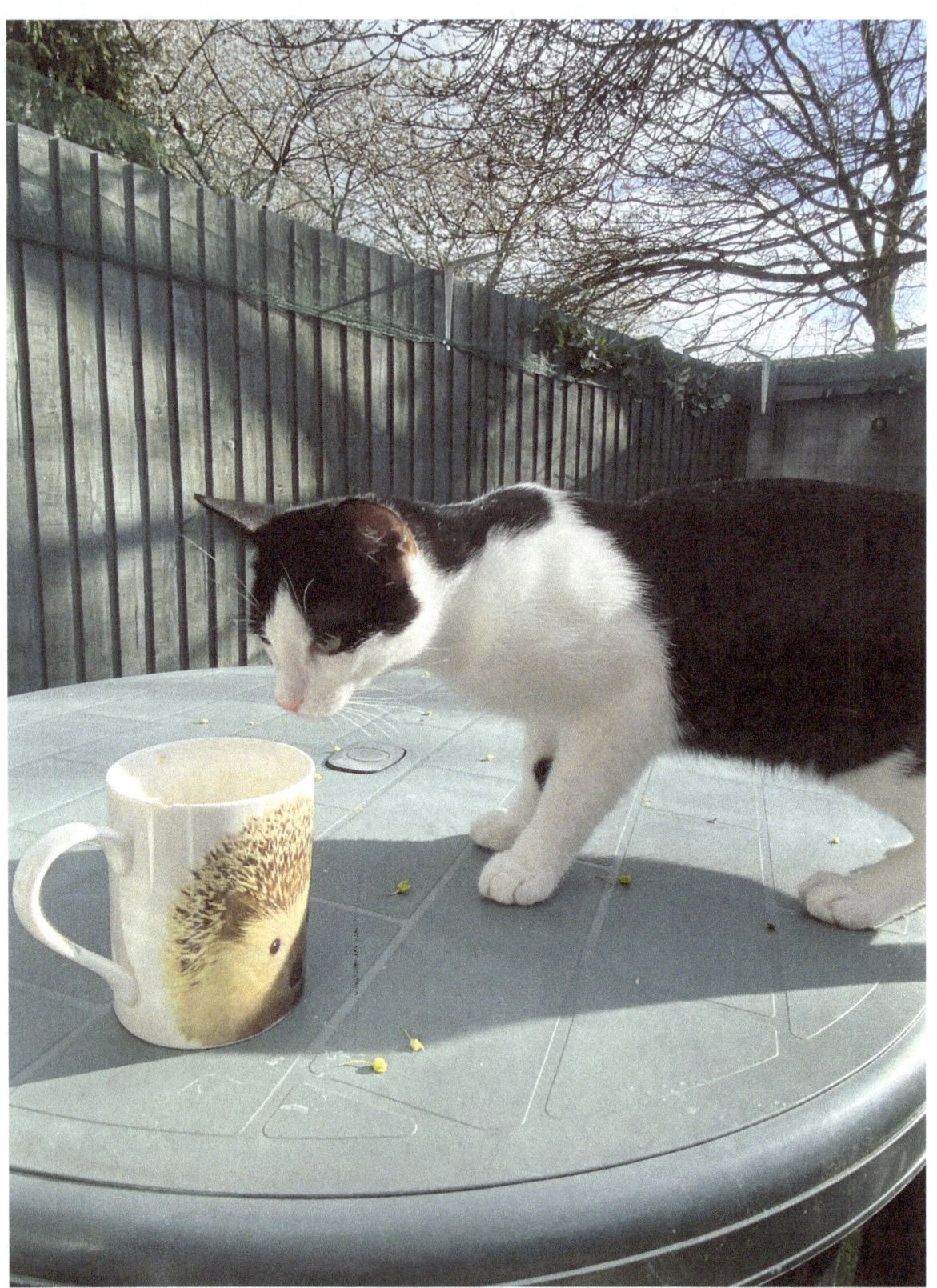

WOW, I HOPE YOU ENJOYED YOUR CAFFEINE FILLED
WHIRLWIND ADVENTURE OF A RIDE WITH THESE
ABSOLUTELY MIND BLOWING PHOTOS OF MY FAVOURITE
THING ON THIS PLANET AND THE ONLY THING
THAT GIVES ME THE WILL TO LIVE.
COFFEE.

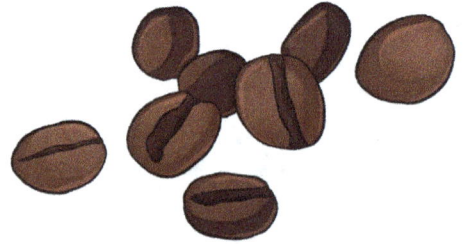